HALF OF GLASGOW'S GONE

HALF OF GLASGOW'S GONE

BY
MICHAEL DICK

GLASGOW
BROWN, SON & FERGUSON, LTD., PUBLISHERS
4-10 DARNLEY STREET

First Edition – 1986

ISBN 0 85174 509 1

© 1986 BROWN, SON & FERGUSON, LTD., GLASGOW G41 2SD
Made and Printed in Great Britain

Contents

Introduction

Having been brought up in the country, I did not have many opportunities to visit Glasgow Harbour as a youngster. However, I do have very vague recollections of a school trip in 1959 to Gourock, when one of the highlights was the cruise down-river from Glasgow. Clearer memories emerged from the early 1960's, when I began to holiday with relatives at Sandbank, on the Holy Loch, and sometimes took the cruise on the *Queen Mary II* from Bridge Wharf or the up-river cruise from Dunoon.

My passion for ships developed during that period and these excursions gave me a very clear picture of the great volume of shipping using facilities on the River Clyde. Trading vessels, of course, were to be seen predominantly in the Harbour but in the general confines of the River there were also ships being repaired; being built; being fitted-out and, sadly, being broken up.

My last cruise down-river in 1969 showed little radical change from 1959 save the demise of several shipyards and the novelty of the container terminal at Greenock. Even then you could not imagine Glasgow being anything other than a thriving port.

In spite of being employed in the Inverclyde area since 1971, for a while I lost track of the changing situation, especially within the Harbour. It was an incident one day in 1982 that led to the subsequent research which made me aware of the current position. Although I had made numerous crossings of the Kingston Bridge over the years, it was only then — and quite by chance — that I caught a fleeting glimpse of the former Kingston Dock, from the south-bound carriageway. It lay far below the Bridge, by the south bank of the river amid an

v

overgrown wilderness. This aroused my curiousity and a subsequent investigation revealed a similar position at Prince's and Queen's Docks and that any vessels at riverside berths were in fact laid-up. The Harbour had certainly lapsed into a state of decline within a relatively short period.

I became determined to recapture some of the atmosphere of what was a lost era, unlikely to return — through photographs, anecdotes and reported incidents. The contrasting view today is presented mainly through photographs and although generally one of bleakness and desolation, there are many aspects which reflect positive developments — albeit not strictly maritime.

For the most part, the content is confined to the period from the outbreak of World War II to 1970. I have made no attempt to give a detailed account of the Port of Glasgow's History, of which there are already publications; and in conclusion, although the Clyde is best known for its steamers and shipbuilding, I have attempted to highlight other aspects of its heritage.

After checking several sources I have come to the conclusion that Glasgow Harbour extends from Victoria Bridge to Scotstoun — a distance somewhat over four miles. I have kept the content, with one exception, to the confines of the Harbour which to me was centred round the two 19th century docks — Queen's and Prince's. The exception concerns Renfrew Ferry and I hope this digression will be excused as the story relating to the Ferry seemed too good to omit.

Of course, the position of Glasgow Harbour now, is not a unique one with similar decline and redevelopment having affected many other ports in the United Kingdom e.g. London and Liverpool.

I must thank the 'Glasgow Herald' for permission to quote freely from stories reported in the 1960's.

Thanks are also due to 'Sea Breezes' for permitting several of their features from 1967 to be reproduced.

Thanks also to the Staff of Strathclyde Regional Archives, Glasgow. for retrieving material and arranging for it to be reproduced in such excellent quality.

My thanks also to the Marketing Department of the Clyde Port Authority for the loan of aerial prints and their permission to publish prints from their collection in the Regional Archives.

John F. Riddell's *Clyde Navigation* was invaluable as a source providing much of the factual information and the plans of Prince's and Queen's Docks.

The 'Appendix of Ships' would have been impossible to collate without using the information recorded in 'Marine News' — the Journal of the World Ship Society. The Central Record of the Society has also proved to be invaluable.

I am indebted to Clyde pilots, Clyde tugmen and towage office staff for their hospitality, co-operation and anecdotes which made this book possible.

Sincere thanks are also due to my wife and family for so patiently tolerating my preoccupation with the book over the past two years.

Any errors and omissions are entirely my responsibility.

Michael Dick
January 1986

SOURCES AND ACKNOWLEDGEMENTS

Newspapers and Periodicals

The Journal of Commerce & Shipping Telegraph; The Glasgow Herald; Lloyd's List; Lloyd's Register; Marine News; Sea Breezes; Ships Monthly; The Scotsman; The Dunoon Observer.

Texts

British Ports and Shipping
Henry Rees
Harrap, 1958

British Vessels Lost at Sea, 1939—45
HMSO Reprint Patrick Stephens, 1980

The Caledonian Steam Packet Co., Ltd.
I. C. MacArthur
Clyde River Steamer Club, 1971

Clyde & Other Coastal Steamers (Second Edition)
C.L.D. Duckworth & G.E. Langmuir
Stephenson, 1977

Clyde Navigation
J.F. Riddell
John Donald, 1979

The Clyde Puffer
Dan MacDonald
David & Charles, 1977

Clyde River & Other Steamers (Third Edition)
C.L.D. Duckworth & G.E. Langmuir
Brown, Son & Ferguson, 1972

Clyde Shipping Company Limited—A History
A.D. Cuthbert
MacLehose, 1956

Empire Ships of World War II
W.H. Mitchell & L.A. Sawyer
Journal of Commerce, 1965

The Golden Years of the Clyde Steamers
A.J.S. Paterson
David & Charles, 1969

Passenger Liners
Laurence Dunn
Adlard Coles, 1961

Sea & River Pilots
Nancy Martin
Dalton, 1977

Steel & Bennie Ltd. Centenary 1856—1956
James Jack Advertising Limited

West Highland Steamers (Third Edition)
C.L.D. Duckworth & G.E. Langmuir
Stephenson, 1967

Photographs

Clyde Navigation Collection—Strathclyde Regional Archives
Clyde Port Authority
Cory Towage (Clyde) Ltd.
Daily Record
George I. Gardner
J. & A. Gardner Ltd.
Guthrie Photography
Laing Homes
Graham E. Langmuir
Lyle Shipping Co., Ltd.
James A. Pottinger
W. Ralston Ltd.
Scottish Exhibition Centre
Studio Clyde (Gourock)—Developing & Printing of Author's
photographs

Personal Accounts

Clyde Pilotage Authority
Clyde Tug Fleets—Clyde Shipping Co., Ltd.
Cory Ship Towage (Clyde) Ltd.

Illustrations

Historical Background

By the mid-15th century, Glasgow had a cathedral, a university and a population of some 2000. The River Clyde was no more than a shallow stream, fishing being the main occupation of the population living on its banks. Goods from the continent were brought to Glasgow by pack horse from the Ayrshire port of Irvine or by rowing boats from ships in the Clyde estuary.

In 1668, however, Glasgow Town Council bought land eighteen miles down-river at the village of Newark which is now the town of Port Glasgow. There was no great demand for port facilities in Glasgow then, as geographically the city was handicapped as a centre of commerce. The River Clyde flowed westwards away from the direction of foreign trade, which as far as Scotland was concerned was then exclusively continental.

The trading position of Glasgow improved dramatically after the Union of the Scottish and English Parliaments in 1707. This opened up the North American English colonies to Scottish traders and the Clyde was in a most favourable situation to exploit the prosperous tobacco trade. From the Clyde sailing ships could make the return voyage to America much quicker than from other Scottish and most English ports. But of course, the lack of deep water in Glasgow hampered expansion and it still meant ocean-going ships had to discharge at Port Glasgow or Dumbarton. With the steady increase in trade and population the Town Council began seriously to consider proposals to make the Clyde navigable up to Glasgow and the varied plans of experienced engineers such as John Smeaton and John Golborne were studied after 1750.

The first Clyde Navigation Act was passed in 1759 and the introduction read:

> Whereas the River Clyde from Dumbuck to the Bridge of Glasgow is so very shallow in several places thereof that boats, Lighters, Barges and other vessels cannot pass to and from the City of Glasgow except it be in the time of Flood or High Water at Spring Tides; and if the same was cleaned and deepened and the navigation thereof made more commodious by a Dock or Dam over the same, it would be a great advantage to the trade and manufacturers of the said City and Parts adjacent and to the Public in general;

Before long, 117 jetties were built out into the river at right angles from both banks. This increased the natural scour of the river and together with dredging, within two years ships drawing six feet were able to berth at the Broomielaw at high tide.

Another major development took place with the coming of steam power. Glasgow and the surrounding area had the raw materials which were in such great demand at that time of Industrial Revolution — iron and coal. Steam dredgers — the first starting in 1824 — and hopper barges coped well with the demands for a deeper river amid the great commercial expansion of the 1850's.

Trade increased so quickly that in 1859 the Town Council decided to separate the affairs of town and port. The management of the port was handed over to a new body — The Clyde Navigation Trust — which was to govern every aspect of the Port of Glasgow. It was to be non-profit making but it had to pay its way.

As the depth of navigable water increased, additional quays were built to provide more berthage, and the Clyde Navigation Trustees realised that sufficient riverside facilities could not be provided to meet demand and from 1867 three major docks were constructed.

Most of the developments in Glasgow Harbour were completed in the period between 1811 and 1914. What had started with the westward extension of the Broomielaw, finished with the completion of Meadowside Granary in 1914 and in that time berthage had increased from some 275 yards to 19,234 — almost eleven miles.

By 1914, only shipyards, on the north side of the river, broke a solid line of quays which then stretched from above Glasgow Bridge to the western end of Merklands Quay, Whiteinch. On the south bank vessels could berth from the Broomielaw Bridge to Govan.

The eleven miles of quay also included the three tidal docks completed in the 19th century and a fourth — King George V — was opened in 1931.

WARRIOR

Cory Ship Towage (Clyde) Ltd.

The busiest and most prosperous time for the Harbour was probably just before the outbreak of World War I and in the year from June 1913 to June 1914, shipping arriving in the Harbour reached a total of 6·9 million tons. Cargoes were varied and sources were world-wide but this was at a time when Britain had no serious competitors for her manufactured goods and exports were booming.

All types of ship were to be seen in the Harbour then:— the transatlantic passenger liners of the Anchor, Allan and Donaldson Lines; cargo liners; tramp steamers; coasters; 'puffers'; Cross-Channel packets and river steamers. Glasgow was emerging as a major European port.

However, by the outbreak of the War, other countries had experienced their Industrial Revolutions and with Britain's commitment to the war effort against Germany, former customers went elsewhere and there was a consequent post-war slump in Britain's trade.

Widespread economic depression in the 1930's also affected shipping very badly and the Port of Glasgow was no exception. The following is an extract from the 'Director's Report' for Glasgow Shipowners Company Limited, which was managed by Glen & Co. It is dated 12th February, 1932:

> The shrinkage in the volume of the trade of the world, which was so marked in 1930, continued during the past year, and difficulties and losses were encountered in the autumn owing to the changes and fluctuations in foreign currencies. Freights have continued at an entirely unrenumerative level and it has been a choice between keeping steamers running at a loss or incurring the expense of laying up.

> The National Maritime Board have now arranged for a small reduction to be made in the scale of wages payable to officers and men, but British tonnage is still handicapped by the lower wages paid in tonnage owned in most other countries.

However, with the outbreak of World War II, there was a major revival in the fortunes of Glasgow. As other ports became more and more vulnerable to air attack, the Clyde became the main European centre of allied shipping. Such was the volume of traffic that Clyde pilots were supplemented by pilots from other United Kingdom ports, and as there was also a severe shortage of Harbour tugs,[1] several London tugs were sent to the Clyde via Inverness and the Caledonian Canal in 1940. These came under the management of the two major Clyde towage companies, the tugs *Sun XI, Sun XV, Contest, Ocean Cock and Racia* under that of Steel & Bennie Ltd.

There is plenty of evidence to show the Port of Glasgow's contribution to the allied struggle and final victory against the Axis powers. On 5th September, 1946, The Clyde Navigation Trust Harbour and Traffic Department released quite impressive statistics:

> The net tonnage of vessels entering and leaving Glasgow Harbour was 97,279,811 and the war materials and commercial goods handled in the same period totalled 51,675,446 tons, all of which was accomplished without serious mishap or delay. The number of troop personnel embarked was 2,136,709 and Service Personnel disembarked 2,441,723, giving a total of 4,578,432.

An indication of the value of the Clan Line fleet to the allied

---

[1] The shortage was made good with the construction of a series of 'Coastwise' tugs from 1941, the design of which was based on the Clyde tug *Warrior*.

cause was the case of the *Clan Colquoun*[2]. In 1942 she left on a voyage which was to last over six months, during which time she travelled over 30,000 miles. In this long voyage, she visited such ports as Capetown, Durban, Bilbao, Newport (Va.) New York, Boston and Halifax (NS.) before returning to Glasgow. On her homeward voyage alone, she carried to this country 64,000 cases of butter, 140,000 carcasses of mutton, 11,000 sides of pork, 1000 cases of frozen bacon and over 10,000 cases of packed goods, all foodstuffs greatly needed at home. Just to complete her cargo she had on deck 13 ambulances and there were also 18 cased trucks and other goods.

By 1941 women were being employed on heavy manual tasks. Modern technology also made industrial work for women more practicable and a precedent had already been set in the 1930's where the developing engineering, light metal and electrical industries had provided new opportunities for women. The war speeded up this trend and many women substituted and worked alongside men in the shipbuilding industry.

The first troop ships came into the Clyde shortly after the outbreak of war. By 1942 King George V Dock at Shieldhall had become a main terminus for the embarkation and disembarkation of troops.

The young, female shipyard workers were, of course, a major attraction for the troops on the up-river passage. I am told that as the yards were passed, the deck rails of the large troop ships were crowded as men responded enthusiastically to the waves of the workers on the river bank. This reaction by several thousand men often caused an alarming list, which was repeated at intervals, first to port as John Brown's Clydebank, slipped by, then to starboard at Renfrew and finally to port at Scotstoun.

This caused some consternation among ships' officers and pilots as many of the vessels had a draught of thirty feet and the River was only some forty feet deep in places. You can imagine by how much a severe list reduced the distance between ships' bottoms and the river bed. Contact or even near contact would have had the most disastrous consequences.

However, before any serious incident took place, a satisfactory solution was found, which probably did not please the

---

[2] Information from 'Sea Breezes', June 1963.

passengers but ensured the ship's equilibrium. While the narrow river passage was being negotiated troops were ordered to 'Boat Stations!'[3]

Strathclyde Regional Archives

TROOPSHIPS, KING GEORGE V DOCK, 1943

Despite such scares, most of the river traffic moved without incident during the war years, although there were exceptions. A tug master recalled the circumstances surrounding a launch in November 1941. King Haakon VII of Norway was due to perform a launching ceremony at Barclay Curle's Whiteinch yard at Scotstoun, the ship in question to be named after the King. She was the second of two sister ships, both dry cargo, built to the order of the Norwegian Government.

The launch was due to take place in the early afternoon at about 2 p.m. but weather conditions, which had been poor, suddenly worsened and soon a dense fog blanketed the River. A British cargo liner, inward bound, had been informed of the hour and place of the launch and had plenty of time in hand to pass Scotstoun before the 2 p.m. event.

---

[3] The problem did not apply on the outward passage as ships carried substantial fuel supplies which provided greater stability.

However, as the King apparently had pressing engagements elsewhere that afternoon the shipyard authorities complied with a late request to bring the launch forward to the earlier time of 1.30 p.m.

Author

PROMETHEUS
Off Gourock, inward bound from the Far East, 1972.

The pilot on board the new ship was not told of the changed arrangements and was astounded when the *Kong Haakon VII* started to slide down the ways. She entered the water and before her progress could be halted struck the incoming vessel causing several casualties among her Lascar crew. It should be pointed out that launches do not usually take place in such conditions.

Although not enjoying the earlier halcyon days the quays and docks were still used extensively in the twenty years or so after the war. The only major change in trading patterns had been the demise of most of Glasgow's passenger liner services to North America but an increase in general cargo handling helped to offset that loss. In 1959, 15 million tons of shipping used the port and some 8 million tons of goods were handled with the dockside assistance of 170 cranes.

PRINCE'S DOCK & UPPER HARBOUR, 1982
Showing area designated for redevelopment

The facilities now provided by the Trust covered a wide range — Dry Docks, Granaries, an Animal Lairage and of course they also maintained a fleet of dredgers, hoppers and ferries. A major new development at the end of 1957 was the opening of Colvilles iron ore discharging plant at General Terminus Quay and the future looked bright with further development plans on the drawing board.

The following list,[4] from a date in September 1962 is representative of the ships using the Port of Glasgow in that busy post-war period. It includes vessels under repair and actively trading.

Berth	Ship	
Custom House Quay	Saint Kentigern	for Loch Linnhe
Broomielaw	Lairdcrest	
	Scottish Coast	
	Lairdsglen	
	Lairds Loch	all for Ireland
Stobcross Quay	Baxtergate	repairing
Queen's Dock	Crane	from Bordeaux
	Paula de Aspe	from Carthagena
	Sunima	from Trinidad
	Baron Inverclyde	from Lisbon
Yorkhill	Sidonia	for New York
Meadowside	American Importer	from Boston
Kingston Dock	Loch Ard	from Western Isles
Springfield Quay	Bhamo	from Liverpool
General Terminus Quay	Hasselo	from Lulea
Mavisbank Quay	Arcadian	from Alexandria
Plantation Quay	Wellington Star	from New Zealand
	Cumberland	for New Zealand
	Manchester Trader	for Vancouver
	Specialist	for West Indies
Prince's Dock	City of Oxford	for Calcutta
	Corinthian	from Genoa
	City of London	for East Africa
	Pacific Unity	for Vancouver
	Colina	for Montreal
	Laurentia	for Montreal
	Gundula	from Stax
Harland's Basin	Corinaldo	repairing
Shieldhall Riverside Quay	Niger Palm	from Freetown
	Doric	repairing
King George V Dock	Nestor	from Kobe
	Suevic	for Melbourne
	Antenor	for Far East
	Lycaon	for Far East
	Clan Grant	from Durban

The last meeting of the Clyde Navigation Trust took place on

---

4   From the 'Glasgow Herald' & 'Journal of Commerce & Shipping Telegraph'.

the 28th December, 1965. The Trust, Greenock Harbour Trust and the Clyde Lighthouses Trust were merged to form the Clyde Port Authority which came into being on the 1st of January, 1966, 'The CPA Confirmation Bill' received the Royal Assent in the month of December and under the Act, the undertakings of the various bodies controlling the River at that time were transferred to the new authority.

In March 1966, a plan costing up to £18 million was the Clyde Port Authority's first initiative since its inception. The main expenditure involved was to be the £12 — £14 million needed to provide ten modern berths in a new dock to the west of King George V Dock — soon named 'King George VI Dock' by the pilots. This would be linked with the progressive closure of Prince's Dock and the general cargo riverside berthage from Springfield to Plantation Quay.

Sadly no new dock materialised but the progressive closures referred to did. New trades, new methods of cargo handling, a huge growth in the size of ships and competition from foreign vessels all contributed to decline by the end of the decade.

The new method of cargo handling was one of the most significant factors in decline. The concept of moving goods in a sealed container transported in vessels, which as someone once put it are only modified versions of the boxes they carry, has many advantages over conventional methods of storing cargo loosely in ships' holds e.g. turnaround is quicker and thus cost-effective; losses by theft and damage are reduced and fewer ships are required. The consequences for Glasgow and other ports were devastating.

With the introduction of the new system, selected ports in the United Kingdom were provided with container facilities to cater for specific routes. The Australasian and Far Eastern services were to be concentrated in the south of England and of course this sounded the death-knell for Glasgow's cargo liner connections with these overseas regions. In 1966 the Clyde's general cargo trade with Australia alone, totalled nearly 100,000 tons. Ten years later it had vanished. Many of these cargo liners had arrived at Glasgow — the United Kingdom terminal — via other west coast ports such as Belfast, Liverpool and Newport and they too were very much affected. However, with the Clyde's traditional commercial and geographical links going back to the tobacco trade of 200 years ago, it was natural to concentrate on the North American container routes.

Container facilities were constructed at Greenock's Princes Pier in 1969 and by March 1973 there were thirteen different services operating to the North American continent. The majority of users were new to the Clyde such as the Johnson Line, Seatrain Lines, ACL, and Hapag Lloyd. Head Line, United States Lines and Manchester Liners merely moved down-river from the Harbour. All the former general cargo services to North America ended.

Author

EUROFREIGHTER
Off Gourock, 1972 as container traffic to North America
was becoming firmly established

These new cargo-handling techniques coupled to new roll-on, roll-off ferry links also had a severe impact on coastal and short-sea trading which was gradually phased out from Glasgow. The last of the traditional coastal cargo liner connections with the Western Isles ended in 1976.

The following list[5] of vessels using Glasgow, one day in July 1972, reflects the developing downward trend in traffic - Custom House Quay, the Broomielaw and Kingston Dock have

---

[5]   From the 'Glasgow Herald'

all closed to coastal shipping. Queen's Dock has closed and Prince's Dock has closed to ocean-going ships.

Stobcross Quay	*Lairdsglen*	from Belfast
Meadowside	*Itapui*	from Rio de Janiero
	Melbrook	from Capetown
	Neddy	from Port Alegre
	Yewhill	from Amsterdam
Springfield Quay	*Lochdunvegan*	from Western Isles
Plantation Quay	*Jalaveera*	from Calcutta
	Port Launceston	waiting
Prince's Dock	*Glen Shiel¹*	from Broadford
	Pibroch	from Islay
	Saint Modan	from Creetown
Stephen's Basin	*Niceto de Larrinaga*	repairing
(formerly Harland's)		
Shieldhall	*Cavtat*	for Yugoslavia
King George V Dock	*Polyphemus*	from Manila
	King Charles	from Beira
	Clan Grant	from Kakinada

The growth in size of ships had a particular effect on Glasgow's iron ore imports when the Hunterston ore terminal was built with the provision of a deep-water berth to accommodate the largest ships. This meant the closure of General Terminus Quay in 1979. It is interesting to note that as early as 1928, Captain Murdoch McKenzie of Glen & Co., Glasgow, drew up plans for an ore and coal terminal at Hunterston. These plans were rejected. He witnessed the opening of the terminal in 1979 but an industrial dispute prevented ships' unloading and Captain McKenzie died before the terminal became fully operational after the dispute was settled.

These changes have affected Glasgow Harbour, in the space of fifteen years or so, to the extent where quays now lie deserted, or have been landscaped; where docks have been filled in and are undergoing or are awaiting redevelopment; where long rows of cargo sheds have been demolished, lie empty, derelict or have been converted for a new role. There are few shipping movements above Meadowside now, and it is debatable if the Port Authority will be prepared to continue dredging for the paddle steamer *Waverley* (presently based at Anderston Quay) and customers of Clyde Dock Engineering at Govan.

---

⁶ Sank about 2½ miles W.N.W. of Ayr, shortly after leaving there 29/6/73 for Glasgow. Four out of five crew were lost.

The current situation is shown by the list of ships accommodated in the Harbour on 18th April, 1985:

Clyde Dock Basin	*Balmoral*
(formerly Stephen's Basin)	
Govan Dry Dock	*Pioneer*
	Robert M
Shieldhall	*Scan Trader*

The decline in shipping movements has had effects other than the closure of dock and quay areas—Clyde pilots have been reduced in number since 1970 from fifty to under thirty; the dock labour force in Glasgow has been slashed from two thousand to just over one hundred; tugs have dwindled in number from seventeen to nine and these are heavily dependent on activities outwith the Harbour for business.

Author

LOCH CARRON
Off Greenock, outward bound for the Western Isles, 1974

At the beginning of May 1984 the Clyde Port Authority reported a loss for the third year in succession. The 1983 figures showed a £1·4 million deficit after items which included £1·06 million for redundancy payments. The Managing Director indicated that the workforce overall, had been reduced from two thousand in 1980 to seven hundred.

Hunterston was the only profitable area of Clydeport operations with coal and iron ore imports well up on 1982. But for
this, the loss incurred would have been substantially greater.
Hunterston, in effect, subsidised the operations in Glasgow
Harbour and other fields. This included Meadowside Granary,
where grain imports were down 100,000, tons, chiefly
because of reduced demand from whiskey distilleries and the
eastern part of Meadowside Quay was to be closed. The
Container Terminal, ironically, had also contributed to the loss
and the Port Authority was seeking further redundancies at
Greenock, where even the three remaining container services[7]
operated by the loss-making Hapag Lloyd company, were in
danger of being lost by transfer to the east coast.

Author

Sludge vessel, *DALMARNOCK,* off Old Kilpatrick, 1984

Among reasons for the decline in revenue in the 1985
Report was the continued drop in traffic to Glasgow. A further
heavy loss resulted in a plea from the Chairman for
government assistance in funding dredging of the Clyde.

Days pass now, without any commercial shipping moving
up-river, even to Dunglass or Rothesay Dock, Clydebank. Not so

[7]   Reduced to two in 1985.

long ago at least two ocean-going ships went up to Glasgow on every tide but the only regular movements are now provided by the daily trips of the sludge boats to Garroch Head and back, and now even they have to pay River Dues to the Port Authority.

The two-thousand ocean-going arrivals in 1972 slumped to even less than two hundred in 1984 and very few of those were flying the British flag. When the Harbour was in constant use it was said there was no water—just oil. Now there is water again and in addition, herons, cormorants, ducks and even salmon.

CUSTOM HOUSE QUAY, 1921

Strathclyde Regional Archives

Custom House Quay

Custom House Quay was opened to shipping in 1852, although it was 1857 before the last section was completed. The construction of this quay, much later than many down-river, was only made possible with the removal of the weir from its original site at the Broomielaw Bridge to the Stockwell Street Bridge further up-river.

MacBrayne's, Burns & Laird, Clyde Shipping and Sloan & Co. did not monopolise the coastal traffic of the Upper Harbour. The coasters of J. & A. Gardner Ltd.[1] of Glasgow also made a major contribution to the short-sea routes of the West of Scotland and Ireland. For many years their vessels plied from the upper reaches to and from such places as Loch Linnhe with calls at Bonawe, Loch Etive and Kinlochleven often with an inward cargo of granite chips

Many of their ships were sufficiently small to negotiate the city bridges, and berth at their usual base of Custom House Quay. This quay was also frequented by 'puffers' and of course the vessels using this part of the River had to lower their masts to pass under the bridges.

A regular arrival at Custom House Quay until her disposal was the small motor ship *Saint Kentigern*. She had been completed in 1937 and when about twenty years old her owners decided to modernise her. Apart from new navigational equipment this also entailed the addition of a monkey island bridge placed above the existing after superstructure.

Just after this work was completed, she was inward-bound and picked up her pilot at Gourock. He had piloted her before the alteration but this was his first experience on the renovated coaster.

---

[1] Still very active in coastal trading.

ARDCHATTAN & SAINT ORAN

It was commonplace, apparently, with Gardner's ships bound for Custom House Quay, that on reaching the Broomie-law the wheel would be handed over to the pilot and the bridge personnel went below for a quick mug of tea before the ship berthed.

This occasion was no exception and the pilot was left alone on the bridge. As the city bridges loomed up the pilot naturally wanted to reduce speed but to his dismay, despite frantic searching, could find no telegraph to transmit his order to the engine room. Fortunately, before disaster struck, one of the crew reappeared on the bridge and pointed out the telegraph unit screwed, to the floor, at ankle level...... Economies had prevented the owners fitting the usual instrument which of course rests on a fairly long pedestal. The crewman was also able to inform the pilot that the telegraph handle, with a bit of practice, could be easily operated by foot control.

Incidently, other pilots using the new bridge for the first time experienced a similar lack of communication.

To avoid striking the city bridges or running aground, it was normal practice to arrive or sail from Custom House Quay some two hours before or after high tide.

When the bridge-wing side light was level with a mark on the quayside wall, it was safe to sail. The usual procedure then, on many of Gardner's ships which were berthed facing up-river was to release the stern rope and the crew go below for refreshments. An incoming tide, surging between hull and quay, swung the stern slowly out into the river in an anti-clockwise circular motion. By the time the tea-break was over the crew surfaced to find the ship had turned through 180° and was pointing down-river ready to sail ahead.

As can be seen from the accompanying photograph of 1921, Custom House Quay, then had obviously played an active role in port operations. The substantial number of berthed vessels, which in many cases are double-banked reflects the popularity of the quay. Although latterly diminishing in popularity, vessels continued to berth there until facilities were terminated in 1966.

I always considered Custom House Quay to be a somewhat neglected area of the Port of Glasgow being tucked away up-river, far from the main activity of the Harbour.

J. & A. Gardner

SAINT FERGUS

Now, the landscaped redevelopment of the Broomielaw extends under the city bridges to take in the old quay. Naturally to accommodate this facility all cargo sheds were demolished and in common with other waterfront changes, there is little sign of its former commercial role.

CUSTOM HOUSE QUAY Looking up-river, 1984   Author

CUSTOM HOUSE QUAY Looking down-river, 1984   Author

The Broomielaw, Anderston Quay & Lancefield Quay

The first Broomielaw Quay was built in the 17th century. Anderston Quay was completed in 1814 and Lancefield in 1840. All, of course, underwent major reconstruction and extension which continued well into the 20th century.

These quays were probably best known for the Irish traffic handled latterly by the Burns & Laird Lines, whose ships were easily recognisable by their crimson funnels, with a narrow blue band and black top. Their ships often monopolised the north bank of the Upper Harbour with the most frequent service being to Belfast.

From 1936 this sailing was by the two sister-ships *Royal Scotsman* and *Royal Ulsterman* which looked like and were fitted-out like mini-passenger liners. From Lancefield Quay they provided six passenger services a week to and from Belfast and were often assisted by the smaller *Lairdscrest,* normally on the Ardrossan—Belfast—Ayr triangle, with cargo and livestock.

The Dublin trade was almost as heavy and in the post-war period, the *Lairdsglen* and *Lairdshill* handled most of it, providing four sailings per week. They were helped by the *Lairds Ben,* which took cargo only. There was also a sailing to Londonderry, on two days of the week only by the 1960's, and handled on the Thursday and Sunday by the *Lairds Loch.*

The 'Glasgow Herald's' 'Arrivals and Sailings' column did not record the movements of the Irish boats, probably because of the sheer frequency and volume of the service. In the course of my up-river cruises to Bridge Wharf during the 1960's, I

THE BROOMIELAW c. 1947

With LAIRDSBURN on the Belfast service; LAIRDSROSE leaving; and on the south side at Windmillcroft Quay Sloan's ANNAN still carrying her wartime lifesaving equipment

Strathclyde Regional Archives

tended to ignore these ships, not being an enthusiast for the coastal and cross-channel types. There was for me, a feeling of disappointment and anti-climax as the steamer approached the Broomielaw—you did not get the same thrill from seeing the smaller ships. I did not even appreciate the delicate manouevres involved in berthing these ships—referred to by the pilots as the 'Broomielaw Cant'.

The reduction in services was very noticeable in the later 1960's. The night passenger service from Glasgow terminated with the sailing from Londonderry on 9th September, 1966 of the *Lairds Loch*, although a livestock and freight service was maintained between the two ports by the *Lairdscrest*. The Glasgow to Dublin passenger service ended on 1st February, 1968 and the overnight Glasgow to Belfast service was withdrawn from 1st October, 1968, although the *Scottish Coast* operated a summer service in 1969. The Glasgow—Londonderry cargo service ceased on the 30th March, 1968 and that to Dublin in 1969...

The passenger services were directly affected by the intro-duction of the new *Lion* which operated between Ardrossan and Belfast from the 3rd January, 1968, and the demise of the cargo trade was speeded up with the evolving 'Euro-Route' of which the Stranraer—Larne ferry service was an integral part.

Now, an extensive and well-landscaped walkway has been laid out along the Broomielaw, the first stage being completed in 1976. It stretches for three-quarters of a mile below Glasgow Bridge to Anderston Quay and the entire length has been landscaped with shrubs, grass and seats, bordered in some spots by white-painted railings. The only reminder here of the area's former commercial use is a narrow border of cobbled quayside and a line of black-painted bollards, adjacent to the river.

Author

CAMMELL LAIRD (ex *ROYAL ULSTERMAN*)
As Shipbuilders' accommodation ship, Faslane, 1968

Author

THE BROOMIELAW, 1984

Queen's Dock

The construction of Queen's Dock, between 1877 and 1880, involved the excavation and dredging of over 2,850,000 cubic yards of sand, clay and rock, all of which was taken down-river for dumping at sea. The dock was built on a site which previously had been a farm and market garden and at the time of its opening was one of the largest wet basins in Britain, taking ships into a water area of 33¾ acres with 3,334 yards of quay.

Originally, dock accommodation was allocated to many of the major companies using Glasgow Harbour such as the Clan Line and City Line and up until the Second World War it was quite common to see horses pulling the smaller vessels in the dock, from their unloading berths, to the North Quay coaling stations to refuel.

A chapter of incidents involved the cargo ship *Empire Puma*[1]; on 7th December, 1941 she had discharged down-river and then proceeded to the Upper Harbour for minor repairs at Queen's Dock. As she entered the dock, her propeller blade struck the side and was badly damaged; later, at her berth, it was discovered that the bondage store of spirits and tobacco had been broken into. The master was held to be liable for this and he was given the option of a heavy fine or a period of imprisonment. After a long spell on the North Atlantic in U-Boat infested waters the captain was inclined to favour a restful time in jail. But unfortunately for him, the naval authorities intervened, the sentence was quashed and the captain was soon reinstated on the North Atlantic. Also, during this time in Queen's Dock, Captain J. D. Ramsay discovered that as a result of a theft from the charthouse, a zig-zag clock, essential for convoy work had gone and he suffered a personal loss when he found that the gold rims had been removed from his spectacles and the lenses left. His visit to Queen's Dock on this occasion was certainly an eventful one.

[1] Purchased from the USA.

26

In these pre-VHF days, private telephone lines were connected between the tugs' base and 'Hailing Stations', which were located at strategic points on the River—Bowling, Rothesay Dock, Queen's Dock, Prince's Dock and King George V Dock. The main qualification for those working there was a loud voice and from these communication points tugs could be informed of their next job, so increasing efficiency.

G. E. Langmuir

TROJAN & *VARNA*
North Quay, Queen's Dock, 1937

Another wartime story was recalled by an experienced tug master, who was then crewing. His tug was assisting an Anchor liner which was preparing to sail and was canting in the Prince's Dock entrance after leaving Yorkhill. As his after tug was 'working round', the stern rope caught and was pulled taut

against the thick, brass lettering of her port of registry—
Glasgow. As the pressure increased the G was removed, then
the L flew off, followed by the A, before the tug was able to ease
off and the rope slackened.[2] After some delay the tug
responsible, headed over to the Queen's Dock entrance to
enquire about the next order. As she hove to, she was hailed:—
"How did things go over there, what kept you?". The skipper
replied with his megaphone: "The job's done all right, but half of
Glasgow's gone...!". You can imagine the effect this had on the
hailer and it must have caused speculation that the tug had got
news of some major disaster that had befallen the city.

A narrow, tidal river channel often presents navigational
problems but the area next to Queen's Dock acquired special
notoriety for its unpredictable swirls and currents. Two
incidents in the early 1960's illustrate the point. The first was
somewhat amusing:—as Clyde Shipping's *Flying Merlin* was
towing a vessel up-river due to berth in Queen's Dock, the cargo
ship suddenly sheered to port and a substantial gap opened up
between the two ships and in the course of the ensuing
confusion *Hopper* No. 27[3] proceeding down-river, calmly sailed
between them, totally unaware that the tow-line was still
holding above her.

The other incident and more serious involved an ore-carrier.
Owing to the deep draught of the ore ships, the timetable of the
journey from the tail of the Bank must be carefully planned to
ensure that suitable tide conditions will prevail at the
shallowest parts of the River. In this instance the ship was
moving up-river on schedule and was due at Queen's Dock
about half an hour before high water. Off the dock, a sudden
swirl caused the large ship to 'sniff' the north bank and the tugs
lost control as she sheered to starboard across the River and
struck Plantation Quay. Fortunately the damage was minimal
but the swirl was probably caused by the characteristics
peculiar to the area. Although another factor which could
influence the movement of ships there, was a release of water
from the sluice above Glasgow Green. Another possible reason
for her 'sniffing' the bottom in this case was an east wind
holding back the flood tide thus reducing the depth of water at a
key point.

[2] A similar incident happened to the emigrant ship *Captain Cook* c 1960
[3] The last steam-powered hopper *Hopper No. 26* went for scrap in 1984.

QUEEN'S DOCK, 1966

Clyde Port Authority

In a press interview after successfully dry docking the *Queen Elizabeth* at Greenock in 1965, her Clyde pilot indicated that there was much more strain imposed on pilots while taking large ore-carriers up to General Terminus Quay in Glasgow.

Author

MATURATA
North Quay, Queen's Dock, 1968

By the mid-1960's Queen's Dock was not being used to anything like its full capacity and the North Basin was often quite deserted save for clusters of obsolete or laid-up hopper barges by the East End. But it still catered for general cargo liner services to such varied destinations as South Africa, the West Indies, the Mediterranean, Spain, Portugal, the Great Lakes, Florida, Canada (West) and the USA (Gulf). By then it was unusual to find more than two or three actively trading vessels berthed simultaneously. Numbers were often supplemented by vessels under repair. Arrivals seldom reached twelve per month but among vessels in dock, reported in March 1967 were:— *Kantara* from Haifa with general cargo; *Letitia* from Halifax with grain and general cargo; Anchor Line's *Elysia* from Baltimore with general cargo and Brocklebank's *Maskeliya* with cooperage and general cargo from Baltimore.

Queen's Dock finally closed to shipping in 1970 and the subsequent purchase by the local authority was soon followed by various redevelopment proposals. These ranged from a maritime museum and a marina to an Olympic stadium and an industrial estate. However, before anything materialised, almost the entire North and South Basins had been filled in with rubble from a variety of sources, including some industrial and some historical. Much of it came from demolished Victorian tenements; St Enoch Station and Hotel finished up there and more recent debris came from the ruined Cathcart Castle.

Author

QUEEN'S DOCK
The final stages of filling-in, 1983

In 1983 I visited the dock in its final stages of filling in. I noticed the road-side sign, yellowish and pitted with dots of rust, at the eastern entrance to the dock, which indicated 'Berths 18 to 32'. Beyond, there were no berths, only a vast, empty, flat wasteland making the area quite unrecognisable as a former dock basin, There was no obvious evidence that this had once been a major off-river wet dock and foundations had already been laid for the Scottish Exhibition Centre.

Over a decade sheds had been flattened, cranes removed and bollards uprooted. Now dust-clouds had been stirred up by trucks en route to tipping their loads into the pool of water which was an apology for the extensive Outer Basin and smoke rose hazily from the numerous, smouldering coup-like fires.

Author

QUEEN'S DOCK
The final stages of filling-in.
The Outer Basin with *BLYTHSWOOD,* 1983

There were still many mushroom-style bollards intact, especially surrounding the Outer Basin and on the north-west quayside, but some in the process of removal had had their squat, oval-shaped upper surfaces lopped off, leaving the hollow, cylindrical base to be disposed of later. On the quay there you could still see the railway line grooves that led to the coaling cranes and mineral quay of the North Basin, and at the dock entrance the main architectural feature of the dock — the Victorian pumping station, to operate the swing bridge and the large cranes, had its basic structure intact though in a derelict condition. Many years ago female textile workers used to take their lunch break, from a nearby factory, at the quayside near the dock entrance and it was dubbed the 'Spinners' Berth by tugmen.

The bucket-dredger *Blythswood* lay alongside the curving section of the North Quay and was possibly the last vessel to tie up there. A dredger was probably the last type of ship you would expect to see berthed in a dock which was almost completely filled in.

J. A. Pottinger

BASKERVILLE
Stobcross Quay in the 1960's

By 1984 access to the dock site was completely prohibited, even the Outer Basin had been filled in and construction of the Scottish Exhibition Centre was well advanced. It was open to the public in September 1985 and officially opened by the Queen in November.

On the reclaimed Queen's Dock site this £36 million development contains facilities for trade or industrial exhibitions, consumer exhibitions, product launches, promotions, seminars, meetings or conferences, sporting events, concerts and displays. A combination of 'spaces' are linked together by a Concourse under a canopy of glass. Parking on site is for some 3,700 cars.

On the riverside of Queen's Dock lies Stobcross Quay, which was built in 1882 and best-known, from 1932, for its hammerhead crane, a major Glasgow landmark. The 175–ton

Guthrie Photography

The Scottish Exhibition and Conference Centre shortly after its completion. The circular building on the bottom left was part of the disused Clyde Harbour Tunnel complex. There are plans to turn this into a tourist attraction.

capacity crane was frequently used by shipbuilders for the installation of engines. It superseded the smaller crane at Finnieston Quay, adjacent to Stobcross. The overall height of the huge, electric-powered crane is some 175 feet and the jib hammerhead 152 feet long.

G. I. Gardner

BAUGNES
Fitting out at Stobcross, 1969

I can well remember seeing the BP tanker *British Bombardier* fitting-out there in July 1962, with the giant crane poised over her after superstructure. From the deck of the passing *Caledonia,* I could make out a group of waving cleaners, high up upon her bridge amidships. In such close proximity she towered above the little paddler, her black-slabbed hull stretching upwards almost infinitely.

One of the biggest single cargoes to leave Glasgow was loaded on board the *Cypress* at Stobcross Quay, in 1967. The cargo, for Chicago, was 17,500 tons of steel coils and plates from Colvilles. The big crane and the floating crane were both used.

Autho.

STOBCROSS CRANE
Standing in 'Splendid Isolation' 1983

Stobcross Quay has now been caught up in the Queen's Dock redevelopment but ships still call occasionally to load heavy lifts. All cargo sheds have now been demolished and the crane stands in 'splendid isolation'.

Yorkhill

Yorkhill Quay was opened in 1909 and became the main centre in Glasgow Harbour for the North American passenger and cargo trade. Both Anchor and Donaldson Lines had extensive services from here before World War II.

An incident involving three large ships took place in the Yorkhill vicinity on 20th February 1961, and was reported as follows in the 'Glasgow Herald':

> The *Circassia*, owned by the Anchor Line was involved in a collision shortly after leaving Yorkhill Quay. She had just sailed for Liverpool to embark passengers and load cargo for Canada, when she hit the bow of Blue Funnel Line's *Jason* berthed down-river at Meadowside Quay. The force of the impact pushed the *Jason* back into the bow of the *Lismoria* in the next berth.
> The *Circassia*, the most serious casualty with a 20 foot gash in her starboard bow, was later towed back to her Yorkhill berth. The *Jason* too had sustained quite heavy damage with a 12 foot hole in the starboard bow at deck level; her stern too was dented. The *Lismoria* only received superficial damage.

By 1966 all passenger provision ended with the sailing of the *Caledonia,* withdrawn from service following the announcement by the Anchor Line that they were discontinuing their passenger trade to India and Pakistan. She left in January 1966, from the Clyde, for Holland where she was to become a floating hostel for the University of Amsterdam. Her older sister ship *Cilicia* had also been sold to Holland for service as a stevedore training ship in Rotterdam.

For a while Anchor, Head and Cunard Lines continued to operate a regular liner service to the east coast of North America, from Yorkhill Quay or the adjacent Basin but again as the container facilities were developed at Greenock the Yorkhill cargo liner services lapsed.

The berths at Yorkhill Quay have been used as lay-up areas for many years now, the most recent occupants being two

J. A. Pottinger

ALAUNIA
Yorkhill Quay in the 1960's

Author

ALBERTWILL & *ORFEO*
Laid-up, Yorkhill Quay, 1983

foreign bulk carriers[1] which had been waiting there, idle for over a year. The rounded rust-stained stern of the Liberian *Albertwill* lay astern of the Queen's Dock pumping station at the eastern end of the Quay. The name and port of registry — Monrovia — were somewhat faded but there were signs of

G. E. Langmuir

FERRY No. 8 & *ALSATIA*
Yorkhill Quay, 1960

repainting work elsewhere. The Greek *Orfeo* was berthed next to the *Albertwill* and was in a similar unkempt condition. Weeds and grass pushed up through the neglected quayside and a reminder of the past, an old wooden notice-board with the tarnished, white-painted words 'Donaldson Line' — indicated the former location of their vessels. The sign was attached to an old cargo shed wall towards the entrance to the quay. Many of these sheds have been renovated and converted for other roles.

---

[1]   Both Back in service 1984

The Clyde Navigation Trust had provided several trans-river ferry services since before 1865 when the first steam ferry was introduced. The last to be withdrawn in 1981, from Kelvinhaugh was No. 8, one of a series of diesel-powered,

MALANCHA

Yorkhill Basin, loading locomotive boilers with assistance of Crane Ship *NEWSHOT* c. 1950

double-ended ferries introduced from 1934. The Kelvinhaugh ferry was located at the eastern end of Yorkhill Quay and No. 8 is now used for passenger trips from Glasgow Road Bridge, Kirkintilloch to Bishopbriggs on the Forth and Clyde Canal and plies as the *Ferry Queen*.

In Yorkhill Basin[2] on 18th September, 1940 the cruiser *Sussex* was set on fire by a German bomb. The master of *Vehicular Ferryboat No. 4*, normally used at Govan, skilfully manouevred his vessel alongside the burning warship so that fire-fighting could be carried out from the deck of the Ferryboat. As a consequence of this successful operation the cruiser's magazine was flooded thus preventing what would have been a fatal explosion.

Strathclyde Regional Archives

VEHICULAR FERRYBOAT No. 4
As firefighter, Yorkhill Basin, 1940

Although there is no active cargo handling in the Basin now, it has played host in recent years to such contrasting vessels as the Royal Navy's *Glasgow*, paying courtesy visits and the mission ship *Doulos*. In 1984 it was occupied on a more permanent basis by an arrested Spanish cargo ship and the laid-up coaster *Pibroch*.

---

2 Completed in 1911

Author

FAIR HEAD
Yorkhill Basin, 1966

Author

PIBROCH
Laid-up, Yorkhill Basin, 1984

Meadowside

Meadowside Quay, below the River Kelvin, was opened in 1914 and became the main centre for handling grain on the Clyde. A granary, built beside the quay, had a capacity for 54,000 tons originally but this was almost doubled after a £3 million development scheme in the early 1960's

A Clyde Navigation Trust publicity advertisement at the time of the extension read as follows:

> The Granary itself afforded storage for 96,000 tons of grain and the sheds adjoining had accommodation for a further 15,000 tons. Delivery of grain in bulk or in bags could be made direct to road vehicles or railway wagons and by band conveyors to smaller vessels or lighters. Nine ships discharging appliances were available at the three berths in front of the Granary and together made possible the discharge of grain at an average rate of 1000 tons per hour, making Glasgow one of the fastest grain-handling ports—ship to Granary—in the UK.

Grain came from ports in Australia, Canada and the USA in vessels ranging from large bulk carriers to general cargo ships with small parcels.

Meadowside has not been without its incidents. A minor accident in 1962 resulted in court proceedings being taken against the Clyde Navigation Trust. The conclusions were reported in the 'Herald':

> Holding that the cause of damage to the bottom of a Norwegian cargo ship must remain a matter of speculation, Lord Kissen in the Court of Session absolved the Clyde Navigation Trust from an action for £4352 damages by the owners of the ship A/S Kristian Jebsens Rederi of Bergen. The owners alleged that the ship, the *MV Brunes* suffered damage to her bottom shell plates, while she was berthed at Meadowside Wharf, Glasgow, in June 1962. They contended the bottom was dented by pieces of concrete or stone, lying on the riverbed at No.2 Berth.
>
> Lord Kissen held it proved that pieces of stone were found in the indents but said there was no evidence that any unusual objects had ever been found in the berth during regular dredging and no evidence of any hard objects or obstructions having been found in the material dredged up.

Author

LEANDROS
Meadowside Quay, 1966

Author

YEWMOUNT
Meadowside Quay, 1969

A thick wall of mud, adjacent to the quayside has often caused navigational problems for ships. On the approach to the quay, vessels tend to stick, almost coming to a standstill. But, although the mud is navigable, many impatient masters want to force a passage through by increasing engine power and are only restrained by the cautious advice of the pilot. Thoughtless action would cause the ship to 'pop' through the mud like a cork out of a bottle; she would then shoot across to the berth with serious consequences for both.

Author

ANANGEL MIGHT
Meadowside Quay, 1983

Meadowside is directly opposite the slipway of Govan Shipbuilders, formerly UCS (Govan) and before that, Fairfield. After a launch tugs must act quickly to arrest the momentum of a new ship and prevent her colliding with the quay. Normally launches pass without incident but a tugman recalled an exception several years ago when all the arrangements and details for the launch had been finalised—the slipway greased and props knocked away. However at the last moment weather conditions deteriorated rapidly but with everything 'set up' perfectly, orders were not given to postpone the launch despite misgivings on the part of the tug masters. In the event the newly-launched ship careered across the River and bumped into Meadowside causing severe damage to her stern.

However, to return to the cargo handling side:—throughout the 1960's grain imports boomed and in 1967 a record cargo of 27,335 tons of maize from South Africa was discharged from the bulk carrier *Kirriemoor* in a little over three working days.

Author

MEADOWSIDE QUAY, 1984
Looking down-river

In the 1970's with the advent of very large bulkers of over 100,000 tons deadweight, many of the cargoes were brought to Glasgow by coaster after transhipment at Tilbury or the other major European port of Rotterdam and traffic generally fell somewhat.

Recently imports to Meadowside have dropped considerably with less demand from the whisky industry, once the major grain consumer. Increased home production of cereals has also contributed to the overall drop in demand. It is a rare sight now to see a bulk carrier unloading and Meadowside barely remains in use as a commercial quay. As I mentioned earlier, the Port Authority has shut down a substantial part of the facilities in order to cut their losses.

Merklands

Merklands Animals Lairage, to the west of Meadowside, was built on Merklands Wharf and formally opened in May 1907. Initially the main trade in cattle was from the United States and Canada but after 1912, strong links were established with Ireland and these were reinforced over the next sixty years to the extent of a complete monopoly.

A tugman recalled the occasions when panic-stricken cattle would scramble over the rails of berthed ships in the course of disembarkation and tumble into the River. Apparently it was quite a sight to see crewmen making attempts to lassoo the beasts before they floundered out of range.

The Lairage, which finally covered an area of about seven acres, had accommodation for 3000 cattle and for sheep and pigs; there were also facilities for slaughtering and cooling. In its latter days the *Shorthorn Express, Frisian Express, Hereford Express*[1] and *Johanna Buitelaar* were just four of the regular coastal traders from Ireland but by the late 1970's the trade had died and since then the Lairage has remained derelict and abandoned.

However, for a spell in 1980/81 the berth was occupied by the *Lancaster,* formerly an Ellerman cargo liner, which was awaiting disposal following extensive damage sustained in a collision at sea. After her cargo was discharged, she lay at Merklands, her forepeak shored up and a gaping hole where her bow should have been. Owing to her owners' bankruptcy the Port Authority assumed responsibility and arranged for the damaged hulk to be towed to Spain for breaking-up.

---

[1] The *Hereford Express* went aground off the Mull of Kintyre 29/10/70 during a voyage from Londonderry to Glasgow and after being taken in tow broke adrift and went aground on the island of Sanda. The 262 head of cattle on board were either drowned or had to be destroyed.

Author

JOHANNA BUITELAAR
Off Greenock 1971, inward bound with cattle, for Merklands

G. I. Gardner

VISHVA BANDHAN
Merklands Quay, 1979

Merklands Quay, just along from the Lairage and also built in 1907 eventually became the main citrus fruit importing centre on the Clyde. Although weather conditions might be ideal, a ship's pilot has to be constantly on the alert as all ships have

Author

MERKLANDS QUAY, 1983

their own idiosyncracies. A good pilot will know the feel of a ship quickly and can sense whether a vessel can handle 'like a tug boat' or at the other extreme will be a 'clumsy cow'. Some ships for no obvious reason, take a sudden sheer to one side or the other and corrective action must be taken immediately. The 'clumsy cow' description could be applied to a casualty at Merklands many years ago and the story is described by T.M. Haddow[2]:

> A foreign-owned 'Liberty' ship was bound up-river, loaded down to her marks with grain. As she was steering very badly, sheering first to port then to starboard and despite the assistance of a head-tug she could hardly be kept on a straight course. This awkward behaviour and the poor response to the helm continued as the ship passed Barclay Curle's Whiteinch shipyard. Eventually she made a bee-line towards a ship berthed at Merklands and the tug made such a valiant effort to pull her round that the tow wire broke. The pilot immediately put the engines full speed astern and both anchors were dropped but these actions failed to stop her progress before she struck the berthed vessel. No serious damage occurred, but insurance inquiries inevitably followed and when interviewed the following day, the ship's master said the pilot was incompetent and had not taken the proper action to avert the collision. When asked at the subsequent inquiry what other action he himself would have taken he was somewhat embarrassed and after some thought admitted he would have done exactly the same as the pilot.

Merklands Quay too, has lapsed into inactivity in the 1980's.

---

[2]   From 'Sea Breezes' May 1967

Bridge Wharf, Clyde Place Quay and Windmillcroft Quay

The quays of the Upper harbour, on the south side of the River, facing the Broomielaw had been operational since 1828, the earlier commercial days of the Clyde. For many years the vessels of Sloan & Company, which linked Glasgow and Belfast with the ports of the Bristol Channel[1], berthed at Windmillcroft Quay.

Bridge Wharf (South Side), which was the name given to the two eastern berths of Clyde Place Quay, lay almost directly below King George V Bridge. It had been the terminus for the daily down-river summer sailings after transfer from Bridge Wharf (Broomielaw) on the building of the last mentioned bridge.

These 'all the way' sailings were operated by the *Queen Mary II*[2] from 1933 until 1969 with the exception of the war years. She left in her earlier years at 10 a.m. for Rothesay etc. with a cruise to the Arran Coast, the 11 a.m. sailing being often taken by the *King Edward* until her departure. After that the *Queen Mary II* left at 11.00 a.m. returning at 7.35 p.m. and called at Gourock, Dunoon, Rothesay and the Kyles of Bute. A once-weekly up-river cruise, performed latterly by the *Caledonia* or *Waverley,* also used Bridge Wharf (South Side) as the Glasgow Terminus.

In July 1961, I set off on my first up-river cruise from Dunoon with great excitement. I was well-equipped for this 'ship-spotting' expedition, having all the necessary paraphernalia, which included binoculars, notebook and pencil.

My uncle had driven me down to the pier from Sandbank for the 11.30 a.m. sailing and he intended to pick me up when the

[1] Final sailing 1965
[2] *Queen Mary* until 1935

QUEEN MARY.

ship returned to Dunoon at 6.40 p.m. However, in the course of the journey he decided that a boy of twelve should not be left unaccompanied on such an adventurous trip and he joined me on board the paddler.

My previous 'ship spotting' activities that month had been carried out from various vantage points such as a promenade shelter in Kirn or the upper deck of Dunoon Pier. At Dunoon you were entertained by the pier record player which played traditional Scottish tunes continuously, if distorted, interrupted only by steamer announcements.

I spent many solitary afternoons there, usually seeing two or three ships and there was often a vessel on trials. Most of these came just within the binocular range necessary to distinguish names but it demanded great concentration to pick out the lettering clearly and you needed to hold the glasses firmly.

I regarded it as a most satisfying occupation but the chance to view the Port of Glasgow at close hand, from the River, was an immensely more exciting prospect and the rewards so much greater.

The first ships were passed at the Tail of the Bank to be followed by numerous vessels at Greenock and Port Glasgow—mainly new-building. It was easy enough to get their names down as ships were of course only on the starboard side. There was isolated shipping at Bowling, Old Kilpatrick and Dalmuir but again you could record names at your leisure. The berthed vessels were supplemented by tugs, coasters and naval craft on passage.

At about 1 o'clock I remember my uncle suggesting we went down to lunch but my look of dismay led to no further developments for the time being. As his hunger pangs increased he made more requests for me to join him in the dining saloon for the 7/6d luncheon. He had always been used to a three course lunch at a regular time and he did not want to break the habit. But hectic shipping activity coincided with his requests and again my reaction forced him reluctantly to give way to his nephew's enthusiasm and what was fast becoming an obsession. In retrospect I find his tolerance was quite remarkable.

The problems really began at King George V Dock, although then I did not have any knowledge of the identity of docks or quays. There was shipping berthed on both sides of the River and on the stocks of the shipyards. I became quite mesmerised as I crossed from one side of the paddler to the other, determined to miss nothing. Needless to say there was a corresponding deterioration in the quality of my recordings.

The most frustrating period was when we passed Queen's Dock and Prince's Dock which were both packed with ships though you could only see masts and funnels behind the obstructing sheds of Stobcross Quay and Plantation Quay.

On our arrival at Bridge Wharf, my uncle was still desperate to get a lunch and we trekked over the bridge into the city but were unable to get anything other than a sandwich as we were too late for lunch to be served.

Author

BRIDGE WHARF, 1984
Showing clearly the clock which was moved
from the North side

The cruise had taken more than two and a half hours and we took the train back to Gourock and the steamer to Dunoon. On my return I immediately attempted to translate my hieroglyphics into English but, sadly, some remained quite indecipherable.

By 1965 there was a considerable reduction in the Bridge Wharf sailings; the construction of the Kingston Bridge led to the abandonment of the berthing facilities upstream by the

Clyde Port Authority but as Glasgow Corporation now owned Bridge Wharf (South Side) from 1967, facilities were still available, and they contributed to the cost of shortening the masts of four Caledonian S.P. Co. steamers. In fact none of them needed this modification as they had ceased to berth above the bridge before its completion, for the end of the 1969 season. The Corporation were unwilling to spend money repairing Bridge Wharf and the service from there was terminated. The Wharf remains as it was in 1969.

Similarly Windmillcroft Quay and Clyde Place Quay have long ceased to cater for short-sea traders but the latter still has a maritime connection as Euro Yachts Ltd. are based there. Windmillcroft Quay is now part of Laing Homes 'Waterfront' housing development with completion scheduled for 1990.

Kingston Dock

This dock, on the south side of the River, was both the highest up-river dock and the earliest, having been opened in 1867. It was a very small basin of some five acres built on the site of a sandpit, and as it was in the Kingston district of Glasgow soon became known as Kingston Dock. The riverside quay, however, retained the name of Windmillcroft.

In its earliest days the largest foreign-going sailing clippers and barques berthed there and the dock had the potential to fit in twenty-two ships of some 500 tons, two deep round the eight hundred and thirty yards of quay. Of course by the 20th century the fifty-two foot wide entrance was found to be insufficient to admit large vessels and the dock began to concentrate mainly on the coastal trade which included china-clay carried in schooners from Cornwall.

In the course of modernisation and during a very warm spell of weather in June 1914, a fire well-fuelled by the timber-constructed wharves, swept round the dock, causing extensive damage. The opportunity was then taken to reconstruct the dock completely and concrete quays were built but it was in 1918 before the work was finally completed.

By 1948 the Glasgow berths for the West Highland ships, previously at Lancefield Quay, had become located at Kingston Dock, the major operator being David MacBrayne Ltd. By the 1950's MacBrayne's older steamers had been superseded by modern cargo vessels such as the *Lochbroom, Lochdunvegan* and later the *Loch Carron* and *Loch Ard*. The voyage of the *Loch Ard* made interesting reading:—from 1955 to 1964 she left once a fortnight on the long voyage to Colonsay, Mull, Coll and Tiree; then westward across the Minch to the Outer Hebrides—Barra, the Uists and to Tarbert in Harris; then back to the ports of Skye and then back to the Clyde, thus continuing the long-established MacCallum – Orme run. During the same period the smaller *Lochdunvegan* provided a complementary service to Lewis and Skye but by cutting out calls at the nearer ports, she completed the service in less than a week. This was the remnant of the traditional Glasgow-Stornoway and Glasgow-Lochinver run, carried out for a long time by such MacBrayne vessels as the first *Claymore,* the first *Lochbroom, Lochgarry* and the second *Lochgorm.*

Strathclyde Regional Archives

KINGSTON DOCK
After the fire, 1914

But it was not only the West Highland ships that used the dock. Many years ago, it was frequented by ships of the ICI company. A regular visitor was the explosives carrier *Cerium.* On one occasion in the late 1950's she arrived off Gourock with serious engine trouble and had come in under tow from Irvine. The pilot went on board and the ship proceeded up-river with the tug lashed alongside. The River passage was uneventful but as the two ships approached Kingston Dock, where the *Cerium* was to discharge her cargo, it slowly dawned on the pilot that there was obviously not going to be enough room for both to squeeze through the dock entrance.

However, a solution to the problem was soon found. The tug slipped the tow and falling behind the coaster prodded and

THE UPPER HARBOUR c. 1960

pushed at her stern. The disabled ship was propelled through the entrance and her momentum carried her across towards the South Quay, where her bow gently touched the berth. A crewman thereupon leapt ashore with a rope and made the ship fast to the dockside.

G. E. Langmuir

LOCHGORM & *HEBRIDES*
Kingston Dock, South Quay, 1951

However, with the introduction of car ferry services to the Western Isles e.g. from Uig in Skye to Lochmaddy and Tarbert, Harris and later from Ullapool to Stornoway in 1964, coastal and general cargo trade declined. The increasing road traffic congestion in central Glasgow and the inadequacy of the River crossings led to plans for the construction of the Kingston Bridge and the eventual closure of the dock in December, 1966. For a while cargo services continued to operate from other riverside berths such as Springfield Quay until they too were terminated.

The old dock became quite a wilderness as I found out on a springtime visit in 1983. The riverside road used to be interrupted at the dock entrance by a swing bridge but that had gone and the road continued unbroken with no evidence of a dock entrance. At this spot, a gap existed between the old cargo sheds and the massive supporting columns of the bridge and it was fairly easy to get access to the former dock area which had long been filled in. I stepped over an almost-flattened wire-netting fence and pushed my way through catkin bushes. With the assistance of a rusting, semi-sunken, lurching oil drum, I jumped over a stagnant canal of water which was choked up with sprouting saplings and other rubbish. Curiously, this narrow water course was adjacent to the old North Quay with its row of bollards, almost hidden by thick tufts of grass. The bollards were quite different from the more common mushroom type to be seen in the Harbour being smaller and knuckle-shaped. The warehouses on the North Quay were quite derelict and in a severe state of disrepair but on the South Quay they were well-maintained and had been adapted for new roles such as the timber centre with its shop front on Paisley Road.

Author

KINGSTON DOCK
The North Quay, 1983

The old Kingston Dock was purchased by Laing Homes in 1984 and after clearing and preparing the site, work began on their private housing development in April 1985. The area will be turned into a base for some two hundred and seventy eight homes, with the first houses completed by the late summer.

The North Quay sheds were demolished in the summer of 1984 and the last evidence of the dock disappeared with the demolition of the South Quay sheds in June 1985.

General Terminus Quay, Mavisbank Quay & Springfield Quay

General Terminus Quay was opened in 1849 as a mineral berth, with rail connections and was used essentially for coal shipments. In 1920 reconstruction work of the quayside from Springfield to Plantation began and the final length of a modernised Terminus Quay was reopened in 1934.

By July 1954, Colvilles took the decision to construct unloading installations suitable for the discharge of ore from two 530 foot long ships of some 16,000 tons dwt. simultaneously. With the expanding Lanarkshire steel industry the established facilities at Rothesay Dock, Clydebank were limited and somewhat inadequate. The old coal-loaders at Terminus were removed and replaced with highly sophisticated cargo-handling equipment. The three meccano-like cranes were each capable of unloading 600 tons per hour and then transferred the ore into the train of rail wagons for the steel furnaces. The new berths were opened at the end of 1957 and later were improved to accommodate vessels of up to 30,000 tons dwt.

Vessels were chartered to the British Steel Corporation and arrived regularly from such ports as Murmansk, Puerto Ordaz and Seven Islands.

There were occasions when an ore-carrier did not arrive at Terminus on schedule. The *Livanita,* which failed to arrive on time, in 1964, had the misfortune to run aground in the Clyde.

Her story was reported in the 'Glasgow Herald' on 30th September:

> The movement of ocean-going ships in and out of the port of Glasgow was stopped yesterday after the Norwegian ore-carrier *Livanita* went aground near the Elderslie repair yard of Barclay Curle & Co., Scotstoun, partially blocking the channel.
>
> The *Livanita* was on her way to General Terminus Quay to discharge a cargo of 23,000 tons of ore when she swung out of the channel. The ship of 26,000 tons dwt. is lying with her bow about fifty feet from the north bank of the river and her stern projecting diagonally into the main channel.
>
> It was hoped to make an attempt with six tugs to pull her off on the afternoon tide. This however, had to be cancelled when it was discovered that the ship had been holed in her forward tanks.
>
> Two tugs stood by her last night and it is expected that a diver will go down to inspect the damage. No further attempt is to be made to refloat her until this afternoon. If the damage is extensive then there is a danger that if she were pulled off she might block the channel completely.
>
> There are already two ships waiting at the Tail of the Bank to make the passage up-river. These are the 7568-ton *City of Coventry,* which is to load a cargo and the *Memphis* of 3575 tons with 700 tons of dried fruit to discharge. A Blue Funnel Line ship was also expected to arrive this morning.

A further report on the 6th October:

> The *Livanita* was refloated with the help of four tugs. About 5000 tons of her cargo of 23,000 tons was unloaded into coasters before refloating was attempted as she had been holed at the bow when she grounded. Compressed air was pumped into her forward tanks to remove water.
>
> She was towed half a mile up-river to King George V Dock and a partial examination of the damage to her bows was carried out by a diver at high tide early this morning. She is to be taken to General Terminus Quay to discharge the remaining 18,000 tons of ore at high tide this p.m.

The excavation of the new dry dock had left very flat rock on the river bed and this was probably the main factor contributing to her grounding, causing the ship to slide to port. In the event, it was probably fortunate that she struck a submerged rock as otherwise her momentum would have carried her on to the dry dock gate. This rock was well charted but did not cause problems to vessels using the dock as they were in ballast.

Another interesting case was in November 1971, when a Liberian ship was due to berth with a cargo from the South American port of Puerto Ordaz. Naturally these deep-draughted ships had to follow a strict timetable on the up-river journey and the voyage of this vessel was expected to take some 4-5 hours. She moved up slowly on the flood tide but at about 4 a.m. as she was passing Dumbarton she grounded in mid-channel. The tide had ebbed some three hours early. She refloated after half an hour or so, but tugs stood by her for twelve hours and no attempt was made at the time to proceed in case further freak conditions developed. She finally berthed at Terminus at 6 p.m. Everyone was quite mystified by this phenomenon, a unique and unprecedented incident. It was later found, after an intensive investigation, that the cause was most likely due to a sustained period of strong easterly winds and this meteorological factor had effected a rapid ebb tide.

G. I. Gardner

ARTEMIS
Berthed at General Terminus Quay, 1979

As ore-carriers quickly mushroomed in size, the Terminus facilities became obsolete and of course, the channel could not cater for laden 100,000 ton ships. To improve efficiency the ore terminal was moved to the deep-water berth at Hunterston, and in 1979 the three cranes at Terminus Quay were demolished and a twenty year-old Glasgow skyline literally bit the dust.

Daily Record

CAPE HOWE & CAPE FRANKLIN
General Terminus Quay, 1973

The bulk carrier *Rounton Grange* could be seen at Terminus Quay throughout most of 1983. In her career she had carried many ore cargoes and must have been by far the largest ship of her type to berth there—and possibly the largest ship to berth so far up-river. But she was laid up and behind her was only a vast, open space, stretching well beyond the quay.[1]

Author

ROUNTON GRANGE
Laid-up General Terminus Quay, 1983

In 1984 the *Grand Encounter* was laid up there. She was on her second spell of idleness in Glasgow. When she first arrived in the Clyde, she could proceed no further than the Tail of the Bank owing to a shortage of fuel. To enable her to reach

---

[1]   Since redeveloped.

Author

SPRINGFIELD QUAY, 1984
Sheds in early stage of demolition

Author

MAVISBANK QUAY, 1983
Quayside sheds were demolished by 1985

Glasgow, Western Ferries' *Sound of Sanda* was chartered to go out to her on two occasions, carrying an articulated petrol tanker. Apparently the master had originally intended tying up at Hunter's Quay pier, but such hopes were dispelled after it was pointed out to him that the facilities there were quite inadequate for the accommodation of 20,000 ton ships.

Just up from Terminus Quay lay Springfield Quay, Built in 1850 and latterly used extensively by the Henderson Line ships trading between the United Kingdom and Burma. It was previously used by vessels of the Clyde Shipping Company. Springfield Quay had not provided berthing facilities for commercial shipping for some time, although on recent occasions barges had been tied up there.

Immediately downstream from Terminus lay Mavisbank Quay, built in 1858 and reconstructed after 1920.

It used to cater for smaller vessels serving the near-continent—France and Belgium—but more recently had lain idle, although its cargo sheds advertised and housed second-hand auto businesses.

By 1985 all sheds on the quayside at Terminus, Mavisbank and Springfield had been demolished and these bare sites will be encompassed within the Laing Homes development.

Plantation Quay

Plantation Quay, fully operational from early in 1875, was immediately popular with the steamships of the Allan and State Lines in the North American trade.

Extensive reconstruction of the quayside was carried out in the 1920's and it later developed into a major United Kingdom terminus for the Australasian trade—New Zealand in particular. In the post-war period, the berths were frequented by ships of the Blue Star, Federal, New Zealand Shipping, Port and Shaw Savill Lines.

Many people will have fond memories of the 15-knot 'H' class ships of the Federal and NZSC Lines. These large, handsome, refrigerated cargo liners, built in the late 1940's brought a cargo of lamb, butter and cheese back to the United Kingdom, after a month long voyage from New Zealand. The New Zealand Shipping vessels had Maori names such as *Haparangi* and *Hurunui,* whilst the Federal Line ships of the class had such English County names as *Cumberland, Huntingdon* and *Sussex.* They made a most impressive sight, steaming light, down the Firth of Clyde after discharging their cargo.

However, the berths at Plantation were not always monopolised by the 'big' ships and the following story relates to one of the smaller units which used the Quay:—In 1960 with dense fog lying in the Clyde area, several ships were delayed at the Tail of the Bank awaiting passage up-river. At about 11 a.m. the fog thinned somewhat and it was felt the River voyage could now be attempted in safety.

Two ships had already set off, when one of the Fjell Line ships from the Great Lakes took on her pilot and weighed anchor. All was well until Bowling but then the fog suddenly descended again and the little Norwegian cargo liner had now to grope her way forward.

W. Ralston Ltd

PORT BRISBANE

Off Renfrew, probably bound for Plantation Quay, 1959

It was 4 p.m. before the ship finally arrived off Prince's Dock and as she was scheduled to tie up at No. 83, the end berth at Plantation, she nosed into the Dock entrance before going astern into Plantation, just round the corner—a sort of three point turn manoeuvre. But just at that moment instructions were received from the Depute Harbour Master to hold position in Prince's Dock in order to allow one of Gardner's coasters, bound for Custom House Quay, to pass safely.

G. E. Langmuir

TROJAN STAR
Plantation Quay, 1935

At first the pilot on the Norwegian ship thought there must have been some mistake as he was certain the coaster had set off from the Anchorage long before his ship. But he was not mistaken and it suddenly dawned on him that he must have passed the coaster, in the dense fog, somewhere on the narrow confines of the River.

By 1970 the days of the 'H' class ships were almost over and many of the other regular visitors to Plantation Quay were being disposed of also. Again the main cause was containerisation and by 1976 there was no general cargo trade from the Clyde to Australasia.

W. Ralston Ltd.

ADMINISTRATOR & *AUTHOR*
Plantation Quay, 1960

W. Ralston Ltd.

CUMBERLAND
A regular visitor to Plantation Quay

The three large ships berthed at Plantation early in 1983 were in ballast and high out of the water. As they glanced westwards occasional trans-river rail passengers or motorists might have been suitably impressed with the bulk of these ships and perhaps considered what cargo they were unloading. But the regular commuter would have seen the same three, day after day, week after week and know they were quite inactive. Their situation merely reflected the depressed state of shipping, world-wide, in the 1980's

Author

MELETE & THETIS
Laid-up, Plantation Quay, 1983

At the westward end lay the black hull of the tanker *Earl of Skye*,[1] recently sold out of the BP fleet. Surprisingly she still retained British registry. Next to her lay the grey-hulled bulkers, *Thetis* and *Melete*[2], but the upper hulls of these Greek sister ships were badly streaked with rust. Their bulbous bows jutted out in front and at the stern, propeller tips and rudder tops cleared the surface of the water.

Plantation Quay, too, is to become part of Laing Homes housing development and by 1985 all sheds had been demolished.

[1] Sailed from the Clyde in April 1984 and made two runs from the Middle East to Europe with oil before arriving in South Korea for scrapping, 28th June.
[2] Both back in service 1984

Prince's Dock

The final completion of what was at first called Cessnock Dock was marked by a formal opening ceremony on September 10th, 1897 and was performed by the Duke and Duchess of York. A change of name also occurred with the royal opening when Queen Victoria, in her Diamond Jubilee Year, gave permission for the 35 acre dock to be renamed Prince's Dock. Construction of the dock was begun in 1893 and it was built on the site of a market garden. It was intended to cater for the general cargo trade and soon began to play a big part in the development of the Port of Glasgow.

One of the most popular lines to use the dock regularly was the Donaldson Line. Immediately after World War II the Donaldson Line discovered it had no ships with passenger accommodation to operate on the Eastern Canada route and after pressure from such sources as the Scottish Tourist Board, for a direct service from the Clyde to Canada, the company converted the two cargo-only vessels *Laurentia* and *Lismoria*[1] to carry 55 passengers. A service which was to last for eighteen years began with the *Lismoria* when she sailed for Montreal from Glasgow on October 4th, 1948.

To celebrate the inauguration of the new service a reception was held on board shortly before sailing. Donaldson's Managing Director, Norman P Donaldson pointed out that the company had complied with the wishes of the Scottish Tourist Board. He added that although the *Lismoria* might not be in the same league as the two giant Cunarders, she was a most comfortable ship and could do something the *Queen Elizabeth* and the *Queen Mary* could not do—that is enter Prince's Dock in the heart of Glasgow and sail up to Montreal.

Two other stories also involved the Donaldson Line's ships directly and their Glasgow base indirectly:— on one occasion

[1]   *Laurentia—ex Medina Victory*
Lismoria—ex Taos Victory

G. E. Langmuir

CELTIC STAR
North Basin, Prince's Dock, 1935

W. Ralston Ltd.

LISMORIA
A frequent visitor to Prince's Dock

the *Lismoria* had left Prince's Dock outward bound and was moving down-river under tow. At Dalmuir the usual procedure was followed when the tow was slipped, but in the course of this normally routine exercise the *Lismoria* carried away not just the rope but a substantial part of the head tug's towage gear. The tug had to wait until her return to the Clyde several weeks later before retrieving her lost equipment.

Another incident relates to a story recounted by T.M. Haddow[2]:

> The incident involved the worst hazard which all navigators have to contend—fog. The Clyde has had its fair share of it, often coming down quickly and sometimes only in patches. On one occasion the *Laurentia* was inward-bound and before boarding her pilot ascertained that there would be no other large vessels moving on the River, and that visibility was clear. Off Dumbarton the head tug made fast and a second tug for the stern was to meet her at Bowling. But before reaching that point the *Laurentia* ran into thick fog and the stern tug failed to appear, obviously held up by the fog. The *Laurentia* was fitted with radar, not a great help in the narrow channel on the flood tide[3], but the head tug was not so equipped. In such conditions—where visibility was so restricted that an officer on look-out at the bow could not be seen from the bridge—smaller ships could anchor in the centre of the River until the fog lifted but this was impossible for the *Laurentia* as the tide was on the flood and if she anchored the following tide would have caught her astern and swung her round. As her length was greater than the width of the River her stern would have grounded, possibly leaving her broadside on across the River. Thus the pilot had no alternative but to continue at slow speed, directing the ship's course while closely watching the radar, compass and riverbank.
>
> Meanwhile, the master of the tug, without radar, could not see a thing ahead and was steering his course by keeping dead ahead of *Laurentia's* bow, knowing she would be using radar. Suddenly he heard a bell ringing ahead, the signal of a ship at anchor in fog and moments later the bow of the *Lairds Loch* loomed up only yards away. She had been on passage up-river when caught in the fog and had dropped her anchor and been swung round by the tide. The tug steered to one side of the Burns & Laird ship but to the master it looked as if the course of the *Laurentia* would take her to the opposite side of the anchored ship and to avoid all three vessels becoming entangled he let go the tow rope. The *Laurentia* grazed along the side of the *Lairds Loch* and finally cleared her with little damage to either ship.
>
> The predicament of the *Laurentia* was now rather serious as a vessel of her size must have a tug to guide her at slow speed.

[2]   'Sea Breezes'—May 1967
[3]   Radar picks up all objects e.g. dockside installations and objects large and small on the River itself. It is unable to differentiate between vessels and bits of wood.

However, by skilful piloting the ship swung round on to her proper course in the centre of the River. While this was going on the 'lost' tug, by sheer good luck regained contact and came alongside the bow of the *Laurentia* and no time was lost getting the tow made fast again.

With the tide ebbing, the riverbanks showed up on the radar screen and despite the continuous fog the pilot was able to take her to Glasgow without a sight of land until visibility improved near Govan. She was safely berthed in Prince's Dock.

To digress, but on the same theme, another incident involving fog was of shorter duration and less complicated but unfortunately it resulted in a fatality. The story again is told by T.M. Haddow.[4]

A large cargo ship was on passage up-river during the night in a clear atmosphere with an officer on watch at the bow and a tug towing ahead as usual. Just before reaching a bend both vessels ran into a patch of fog lying across the River, but it did not reach any great height, and while it completely enveloped the tug, the bridge of the ship high above was not affected. From it could be seen the lights on the riverbank which were also above fog level, and the ship was steered round the bend simultaneously with her charge, in consequence of which the tow rope went momentarily slack and then suddenly taut again. The jerk caused the rope to snap, resulting in one end rebounding towards the large ship with terrific force and a steel shackle attached to the rope struck the head of the officer at the bow, killing him outright.

As ships got bigger the South Basin of Prince's Dock began to present very serious navigational problems[5]. The knuckle corner of the South Pier acquired particular notoriety owing to the restricted room for manoeuvre and was nicknamed 'Tattenham Corner' by the tugmen and 'Hell's Corner' by pilots.

A tugmaster recalled the time in the 1950's when he was taking a ship out, laden with a cargo of large pipes for South America. Ships were berthed to port and starboard including the corner berth and there was barely two feet to spare on either side as the tugs delicately edged the vessel out.

Further evidence demonstrating the difficulty in coping with the congestion of the South Basin was provided by the pilot of a Greek ship more than twenty years ago. It was early in the day, about 7 a.m. as the vessel entered the dock and began to make the gradual, sweeping turn into the Basin. Unfortunately difficulties arose resulting from some erratic steering. The helmsman did not make an adequate allowance for the turn

4 'Sea Breezes'—May 1967
5 See diagram of Dock plan

PRINCE'S DOCK, QUEEN'S DOCK & UPPER HARBOUR, 1960

and she approached at too tight an angle and struck the knuckle of the South Pier. At this point the ship's master evidently suffered a breakdown and resorted to the refuge of his rosary beads which unfortunately were unable to prevent further mishaps. The ship then sheered to starboard and collided with the South Quay, narrowly missing a berthed cargo liner. At this stage the master apparently went beserk and directed his wrath at the pilot: "You bloody fool, what for you put my ship here?", he screamed. A torrent of abuse followed and stevedores and the ship's agent on the quayside were astounded as the stream of oaths and curses emanated from the bridge of the ship above them. But the pilot calmly completed his task and the ship berthed eventually.

It later transpired, however, that the ship had previously docked at Aberdeen where she had experienced similar pre-berthing problems. So not all the blame could be attributed to the design hazards of Prince's Dock's South Basin.

With the deepening of the navigable channel in the Clyde, there was a great upsurge in shipping on the River. Big shipping companies came into being and began trading world-wide. These shipping companies wished to engage pilots known to them and a class of 'special' or 'choice' pilots came into being and continued on the Clyde until fairly recently.
During a six week tug strike in 1962 the only method of keeping the Port open was for pilots only, to take the ships up-river. The Ellerman City Line's 'special' pilot at that time, Captain John Taylor, in particular, gained a reputation for skilful berthing. In the dock entrance of Prince's, the starboard anchor was dropped and allowed to run out while the ship continued ahead. When the anchor had run out to about nine shackles or eight hundred feet, the vessel, in mid-dock was completely stopped. She then heaved on the starboard anchor which pulled the bow to starboard, bringing the ship into a position to move neatly into one of the company's North Quay berths in the North Basin. Generally at this time to facilitate berthing the corner berths at Prince's Dock were kept clear of shipping.

An amusing incident happened many years ago and was recalled by Captain Ian Clark who was piloting a Panamanian vessel of some 3000 tons—the maximum before tugs were required. She was to berth in the Centre Basin which would be quite a tight sqeeze as the corner berths were occupied so

W. Ralston Ltd.

PRINCE'S DOCK & QUEEN'S DOCK, 1960

leaving little room for manoeuvre. She moved slowly through the dock entrance and started to swing round into the Basin. The pilot, on the port wing bridge, gave instructions to go 'Slow Astern' But there was no response from the engine room and she continued to drift on, maintaining her course. A further order of 'Half Astern' failed to meet with any response and on

G. E. Langmuir

WINGA & *CITY of OTTAWA*
Berthed at western end of Prince's Dock, 1960

investigation the pilot was horrified to find the wheelhouse deserted. The entire bridge watch were out on the starboard bridge wing peering through binoculars. They had been totally distracted by a young lady, scantily clad, at one of the windows in a nearby Govan tenement[6]. The pilot drew their attention to the situation and an evasive turn of the wheel to starboard prevented an imminent collision with the South Pier.

In 1964 Prince's Dock's quays were lavishly equipped with sixteen three-ton cranes and six six-ton electric cranes. The dock at this time generally retained its popularity unlike its Queen's Dock neighbour.

Services were provided to South Africa, East Africa, West Africa, Pakistan, the Persian Gulf, East Canada, West Canada, South America and the Great Lakes.

6   The aerial photographs show the extent of tenement housing at that time.

In a typical month, March 1967, there were over twenty arrivals. Among these were:—Henderson's *Yoma* from Rangoon with general cargo; Runciman's *Hazelmoor* with general cargo from Bombay; Ellerman's *City of Philadelphia* with general cargo from Bombay; Ellerman's *City of Swansea* with general cargo from East Africa; Donaldson's *Santona* from St. John with general cargo.

Strathclyde Regional Archives

PRINCE'S DOCK
Fire damage to Shed C, Berth 12, Centre Basin 1962

Incidents have included the serious fire in the North Pier sheds in 1962 and in the great gale of 1968 tugmen were called out to duty when a ship fitting out in Stephen's Basin, was in danger of breaking her moorings. They reported to the tug in Prince's Dock only to find the water lapping over the bollards.

Again containerisation gradually spelled out the end of Prince's Dock as an active cargo-handling area and the dock closed to ocean-going ships on 2nd July, 1971. Small coasters continued to use the West Quay for some time after and the Isle of Man Steam Packet Co's *Mona's Isle,* on the Clyde for a refit by Clyde Dock Engineering, occupied a berth there in the winter of 1984-85.

PRINCE'S DOCK
Looking across to Queen's Dock, 1962

The three basins of Prince's Dock had been filled in almost completely when I made a recent visit in 1983 but there was still plenty of open water remaining to tip rubbish into, where the former canting area was, at the western navigational entrance. Some quayside installations[7] were still in situ e.g. five cranes and most cargo sheds were intact on the old Piers. One trio of cranes on the North Pier dominated a pile of assorted junk.

Author

SOUTH BASIN, PRINCE'S DOCK, 1983

Beyond the cargo sheds and towards Plantation Quay you could see the sloping-topped funnels and bridge structure of the two large, laid-up bulk carriers and the red funnel of the old tanker *Earl of Skye*.

In 1983 the area was purchased from the Clyde Port Authority by Laing Homes, who hope to attract people back into the inner city area—a reversal of recent trends—with an attractive housing complex which includes a landscaped marina towards the dock's western end.

However, in November 1984, it was announced that the

7   The cranes were all toppled by July 1984 and the site was completely cleared by 1985.

Clyde Port Authority

PRINCE'S DOCK
Looking across to Queen's Dock, 1962

Government had chosen Prince's Dock as the venue for Britain's third National Garden Festival in 1988. It will run for five months from April to October and is expected to attract more than three million people.

Author

THE CENTRE BASIN, PRINCE'S DOCK, 1983
Looking towards the North Pier

After lengthy negotiations Laing Homes, the owners, leased the site to the Scottish Development Agency, who will stage the Festival. Most of the area will revert to Laing for private housing in the early 1990's. One of the most spectacular ideas is the plan to create a bridge link to the new £36 million S.E.C. along with a walkway on the south bank of the Clyde.

Silt from the Clyde riverbed is to be used to help provide topsoil for the Festival.

Author

PRINCE'S DOCK, 1983
Looking across the canting basin
towards North Quay, North Basin

Author

SOUTH BASIN, PRINCE'S DOCK, 1983
Looking towards the East End

Laing Homes

MODEL, INDICATIVE OF HOUSING PLAN FOR PRINCE'S DOCK c. 1990

Govan Dry Docks

Just to the east of Govan, the Clyde Navigation Trustees decided to construct a graving dock 500 feet × 60 feet so as 'to answer fully all the requirements of such a great shipbuilding port as Glasgow'. On 11th December, 1875 the first vessel entered the new dock which soon proved to be the most popular with both shipowners and shipbuilders; a second opened in 1886 and twelve years later, a third.

There was an unfortunate accident in 1961 which had a most interesting sequel. This happened in No. 1 Drydock on Saturday, 17th June and was reported as follows in the 'Glasgow Herald':

> Masonry and part of the railing at the front of the dock were embedded in the damaged bow of the Court Line cargo ship *Jevington Court* after the ship rammed the side of the drydock when it flooded. When the accident occurred the ship had just been towed into the dock for routine repairs—scraping and painting.
>
> The caisson-dock gate—which was about 32 feet high, 50 feet long, 12 feet wide and slightly wedge-shaped, had been towed into position and lowered. The water inside the dock had been nearly pumped out when the caisson jumped up and was thrown inwards striking the ship, under her stern.
>
> The incident took place just before high tide. The ship's bows smashed against the head of the dock, splintering a flight of stairs to fragments; a large quayside coping stone was embedded in a 10 feet × 4 feet gash in the bow.

For many years, the Clyde pilots had been trying to amend an old byelaw which went back to the 19th century. At that time, when communications were poor, the byelaw ruled that inward pilots—Gourock to Glasgow—must reside within half a mile of Gourock pier, where the pilot station was located. This was to make it easier to get in touch with the pilot quickly. Outward pilots—Glasgow to Gourock—had to reside within half a mile of the River between Renfrew and Glasgow Bridge. Of course by 1960 with good roads, motorised transport and telecommunications the byelaw had become something of an anachronism.

In 1961, an 'inward' pilot based in Gourock, was promoted to Glasgow. When Glasgow pilots retired, the senior pilot at Gourock in turn transferred to the City. There was a great advantage in this move as there was no stand-by duty in a pilot station awaiting the arrival of ships. Neither was there the inconvenience of a night in the 'dunney' at Clyde Trust headquarters when the last train to Gourock had gone.

The departure time of ships in the docks are usually known well in advance and so pilots had plenty of warning before their next turn so they could stay in their homes until shortly before sailing time.

MASKELIYA   Author
In No. 3 Govan Dry dock, 1966

In accordance with this byelaw, the newly promoted pilot prepared to take up residence in the Glasgow area. He took up the new appointment but in the short period before finding suitable accommodation in Glasgow he had permission to travel from Gourock when his services were required. His car was always kept immediately in front of the house ready for the quick dash to Glasgow.

He was 'on call' at the time of the *Jevington Court* accident and on receiving his orders sped off in the evening to Glasgow. He arrived at Govan ten minutes before the Harbour Master, who had only to come up from Scotstoun. Needless to say the archaic byelaw was repealed soon after.

The dry docks are now owned by Clyde Dock Engineering Ltd, who began operations on 4th April, 1977. The company had taken over the ship-repairing facilities of Alexander

Stephen—Stephen's having earlier purchased the docks from the Trustees.

Apart from the short spell in 1981 when Clyde Dock was put on a 'care and maintenance' basis, its order book has been very healthy. The Company has done well to survive in what is a

Author

No. 3 GOVAN DRY DOCK, 1984

highly competitive industry. Sea Link ferries operating on the Stranraer-Larne route are regular customers but larger cargo ships have been repaired and recent work has even included the conversion of a ship for Ministry of Defence work. Although too big for the drydock, the 'Panamax' bulk carrier *Irish Spruce* recently received engine repairs.

Stephen's Basin

Immediately down-river from the Govan Dry Docks was Harland and Wolff's (originally Napier's) fitting-out basin. It measured 600 feet × 180 feet and could accommodate ships of up to 11,500 tons d.w.t. However it was announced on 22nd October, 1963, that Harland and Wolff were taking steps to place on a 'care and maintenance' basis their ship-building and ship-repairing yard at Govan.

This yard was developed from the yards of the London and Glasgow Iron Shipbuilding Co., Ltd. (formerly Smith & Rodger) and Mackie and Thomson Ltd. (formerly Mackie and Thomson) which were purchased by Harland & Wolff Ltd. in 1912.

When they discontinued their shipbuilding activities, Alexander Stephen and Sons Ltd. acquired the wet dock and used it essentially for ship repair business. On 3rd March, 1966, Glasgow Corporation agreed to buy the former shipyard for redevelopment.

Author

SIR GALAHAD, fitting out & *CORINTHIC*
repairing Stephen's Basin, 1966

In October 1966, there was an incident involving the Clyde Shipping Company's tug, *Flying Dipper* in the basin. The story was reported in the 'Herald':

The *Flying Dipper* sank on October 18th in Stephen's Basin after being holed in a collision with the Shaw Savill cargo liner *Doric*. The collision occurred when the tug approached the *Doric* which had been undergoing repairs since August, to take her in tow. She backed in and lay alongside. The *Flying Dipper* was struck by one of the *Doric's* twin propellers towards the stern. The engine room immediately flooded and the propeller, according to one eye-witness 'had cut through the hull as a knife through butter'. She returned to the Basin, where her crew climbed ashore before she sank. Skilful manouevering had averted what might have been a very nasty situation. Had the *Dipper* sunk in the Channel she would have been a major obstruction to shipping.

And a further report:

...Salvage operations took about six weeks. She was raised on 9th December, 1966 with difficulties arising because of working in mud and also because the craft was extremely heavy in relation to her size.

Camels-circular buoyancy tanks-were sunk in position around the tug and then pumped out with compressed air to lift the tug. The salvage vessel *Succour* assisted in raising her at the stern.

Stephen's ceased shipbuilding and ship-repairing at the end of the 1960's and the Basin was later taken over by Clyde Dock Engineering Ltd.

CLYDE DOCK BASIN, 1984   Author
(formerly Stephen's)

Shieldhall

In 1927, a 227 yard length of quay was completed which joined the north-east corner of King George V Dock to the old wooden wharf at Shieldhall. The new Riverside Quay was extended further in 1958 and equipped with six × 10 ton electric cranes. It was first used for timber imports and other bulk cargoes but the export of steel coils became a later speciality.

Author

TARRY
Lying arrested, Shieldhall Quay, 1984

Part of the old, wooden wharf still remained, adjacent to the new quay and several years ago, in thick fog, a tug crashed into the wharf head-on. The result was an indentation, almost large enough to accommodate the entire tug and it became a well-known local landmark, named 'Peterson's Hole'—after the unfortunate tug master.

The only opportunity the tug *Flying Fulmar* has had to use her fire-fighting equipment was in 1979 during a timber fire at Shieldhall but she was unable to take advantage of this unique occasion and could not contain the blaze which was finally extinguished by land-based fire engines.

Author

EARL OF SKYE
Off Shieldhall, outward bound after lengthy period of lay-up, 1984

Further up-river from the Riverside Quay, but still in the Shieldhall location, a berth has been provided for many years for one of the two sludge vessels now operated by Strathclyde Regional Council. One story referring to the older days of these ships is recounted by T. M. Haddow:[1]

> The Clyde has a bad reputation for fog. Having to make the outward and inward trip every weekday throughout the year, the masters of the sludge vessels have an excellent knowledge of the river and in consequence conditions have to be very bad to stop them sailing. In recent years these ships have been equipped with radar, but before that aid became available they had their own 'detective' methods of knowing their position when nought could be seen and steering was by compass only.
>
> When thousands of rivets were used in the construction of ships, down-river progress from Shieldhall could be followed by the noise of the riveters at work in the various shipyards;

[1]   'Sea Breezes Feb. 1967

Connell's, Blythswood and Yarrow to starboard: Simons Lobnitz to port followed by John Brown's to starboard. Other recognisable sounds were the outflow of water from Dalmuir Sewage Works and from the canal lock at Bowling and the chains of the Renfrew and Erskine Ferries.

Author

ANTIPOLO I
Being towed from King George V Dock to Shieldhall Quay, 1984

To judge the ship's distance from either bank of the River, it was the custom to throw out lumps of coal. A splash indicated that there was water as far as one could throw but if a thud was heard, it served as a warning to 'move over a bit'. The invention of radar was timely as now silent welding has replaced riveting and no coal is available as the ships burn oil.

Shieldhall Quay is still in occasional use but has recently accommodated laid-up or arrested vessels. One such case involved a Phillipine cargo ship which was moved from King

George V Dock in April 1984, to Shieldhall.[2] The circumstances of her arrest and subsequent position were reported thus in the 'Glasgow Herald' on the 30th June, 1984:

> Ten Fillipino crewmen and their ship have been stranded in Glasgow for three months because of a legal wrangle over a shipping company's debts and the condition of a cargo of sugar.
>
> Since her arrival, the Phillipines registered *Antipolo I* has collected twenty one writs from various parts of the world. Mr Reynaldo Santa Ana, the captain, said yesterday: "All we want to do is go home. We have been here for ninety-two days waiting for orders. There are court hearings just about every day but we hope to be on our way by the middle of next month".
>
> The *Antipolo I*, owned by a Manila-based firm, had arrived in Glasgow to uplift machinery from Babcock and Wilcox for transport to Hong Kong.
>
> However as she lay in the King George V Dock, Govan, the creditors caught up with her.
>
> The principal creditor is the Banque Indo Suez in Manila, which according to the initial writs, is claiming 3,468,000 dollars, nearly four times the estimated value of the ship.
>
> Last month the Bank's application for a warrant for the ship's arrest was granted by a Glasgow Sheriff as the ship was in Scottish jurisdiction. The bank was then entitled to dispose of the ship once the cargo had been removed.
>
> However, a 3000 ton load of sugar was condemned by port health inspectors who claimed it had been infested by rats.
>
> That meant the unloading had to stop.
>
> Yesterday Glasgow Sheriff Court was considering an action by the Egyptian firm awaiting the sugar in Port Said—they want the sugar for making jam—against Glasgow District Council.

---

[2] After part-unloading the vessel moved back to KGV and the situation was not resolved until December 1984, when she finally left the Clyde.

King George V Dock

Since the opening of the dock in 1931, general cargo liners have sailed in regularly from Australia, Japan, South and East Africa and the Red Sea. The dock was to cater initially for the Blue Funnel Line but it was hoped that some of the passenger liner services based up-river would make use of the vast new dock. Unfortunately the opening coincided with the world depression and custom did not materialise as expected.

The wartime importance of Glasgow Harbour has already been stressed but King George V Dock was to have a particularly important role. Its expanse and deep-water offered excellent facilities for almost the largest ships both merchant and naval. In April 1942 the United States Navy aircraft carrier *Wasp* came up to King George V Dock and took on board a large number of Spitfires, sailing immediately for an unknown destination. On 20th April the *Wasp* was heading for Malta, then in its most desperate plight. When the *Wasp* was still fifty miles away, an attack on the island developed. The Spitfires at once took off and descended on the attackers like a bolt from the blue, practically wiping them out.

King George V also provided a welcome haven for a tanker in 1941[1]. The oil tanks at Old Kilpatrick were set on fire during the night of the Clydebank Blitz on the 14th March. At that time, a large Norwegian oil tanker the *Ferncourt* was berthed at the adjacent jetty but was in no immediate danger. The River, then, was completely closed to shipping because of the large number of unexploded mines.

On 15th March, however, the wind changed direction and there was a great risk of the tanker catching fire. The tugs *Warrior, Chieftain* and *Racia* were sent from Greenock to rescue the threatened vessel but owing to faulty communication, they were stopped by the River Patrol from proceeding further than Dumbarton.

[1]   From 'Steel & Bennie Centenary'

After returning to Greenock they were again dispatched to the assistance of the *Ferncourt* and they arrived alongside the tanker with the tide ebbing strongly. As flames were sweeping across the wharf, the pilot was unable to board the *Ferncourt* from the shore but the master of the *Warrior,* Malcolm MacIntyre, then volunteered to pilot the ship to Glasgow. The *Warrior* and *Racia* made fast ahead, the *Chieftain* made fast astern and they set off on the hazardous passage up-river.

At about 5 p.m. when off Renfrew Pier, a land-mine exploded underneath the *Warrior* with such great force that she was lifted almost clear of the water. The *Chieftain* slipped the tow and went to aid the stricken *Warrior,* leaving the *Racia* which had also suffered some minor damage to keep ahead of the ship. But the *Ferncourt* had sheered violently under the impact of the explosion and was making straight for the Renfrew Ferry slip.

Skipper MacIntyre used the ship's engines cleverly and steered clear of the slipway and continued up-river, berthing safely in King George V Dock—with one tug. The operation had involved a great feat of seamanship as the tanker was almost five hundred feet in length.

In the meantime the *Chieftain* had assisted the *Warrior* alongside the collapsed pier at Renfrew, where she sank after the crew were taken off. Eventually she was lifted and refloated. On 25th March after being examined in Queen's Dock, it was found that her machinery had been badly damaged and for the most part was irreparable and there had also been some hull damage. She was towed to Port Glasgow and returned to service on 12th October.

Also during the war years there was a nasty incident involving the troop ship *Nea Hellas* as she was leaving King George V Dock on the ebb tide, probably for dry docking. She broke contact with her tugs, went out of control and when off Shieldhall became straddled broadside across the River, blocking the Channel completely. Both bow and stern grounded and it required the help of some 13 tugs to refloat her on the next tide. She suffered some stern damage but the efforts of the tugs ensured no major hold-ups for shipping movements.

The *Nea Hellas* was an interesting vessel having started her career as the Anchor Line's *Tuscania* and built for the Clyde–New York service. But during the summer months of the years 1926-30, she operated on Cunard's London–New York trade, spending those winters on the Anchor Line's Indian services. Late in 1931 she was permanently transferred to the latter and sold to the Greek Line in 1939. She was taken over by the British Government for trooping during the war when she was affectionately and unofficially rechristened *Nellie Wallace*. After the war she was returned to her former owners in 1947 and was engaged in the North Atlantic emigrant trade under the name *New York*.

Strathclyde Regional Archives

BARNEY KIRSCHBAUM
Unloading US jets King George V Dock, 1948

There was an interesting arrival[2] in Glasgow in 1948 when the first seventeen of the United States jet-propelled Shooting Star fighter planes on their way to form part of an operational fighter group in Germany were unloaded.

The aircraft were carried as hold cargo in the American Army Transport *Barney Kirschbaum,* which lay in King George V. Tractors towed the planes, which were more or less

---

2   From the 'Scotsman'

completely assembled, to nearby Renfrew Airport, where they were made ready for flight and tested before taking off for their German base in the US zone.

Cory Towage (Clyde) Ltd.

FORAGER

On 23rd May, 1962 just down-river from 'KG Five', as the dock became popularly known, a fatal accident took place. It was reported in the 'Herald':

> The tug *Forager* may have been pulled under by a hawser that held when subjected to exceptional stress which normally would have caused the tow to part. The *Forager* sank at Scotstoun as she was assisting a New Zealand cargo liner, the *Hororata*[3] up-river to Plantation Quay.
>
> According to a crew member the *Forager* had been at the stern of the *Hororata* when her wash began to pull the tug round. But the hawser did not break and held until the tug was lying abeam the ship's wash and the tug began to list to starboard. In the event two men drowned.

A further report:

> The *Forager* was raised on the 6th June 1962 and roped to the grab hopper *Lennox II* and taken to King George V Dock. The River Channel between King George V Dock and Renfrew Light was

[3]   The tug *Iselgarth* owned by R & J H Rea sank off Penarth 15/1/66 after coming into contact with *Hororata* during berthing operations. Three crew members lost their lives.

closed from 6 a.m. until noon to allow the tug to be raised and the operation was completed on schedule.

Because of the salvage work, the steamer *Queen Mary II,* which was sailing from the Broomielaw with 600 OAP's on a day's outing to Dunoon and the Kyles of Bute was slightly delayed. The steamer had to tie up at Shieldhall until the Channel was clear.

My interest in ships began in the late 1950's when I became aware of the ex-LST's[4] laid up in the Holy Loch, while holidaying with relatives from Sandbank. For many years from the age of twelve or so, I made my own way to Cowal from my Perthshire home by train and boat, at both Easter and summer.

J. A. Pottinger

THESEUS
King George V Dock, in the 1960's

It was always an exciting moment to catch the first glimpse of ocean-going ships berthed in the Upper Harbour, as the train pulled out of Platform 13 at the Central Station and crossed the Clyde. There were no further opportunities to view shipping until the train reached Hillington. If you looked to the right there, you could see 'KG Five' some distance away over fairly open countryside; the ships looked as though they were

4   Landing Ship Tank

Strathclyde Regional Archives

CLAN SHAW & AENEAS
King George V Dock, 1950

berthed in a field such was the lack of industrial development then. The dock appeared to be the exclusive domain of the Blue Funnel and Clan Lines. Amidst the indistinct mass of derricks, masts and dockside cranes, you could pick out the lofty 'Blue Flues' mixed with the squatter funnels of the Clan Line ships. There might also be a solitary Shaw Savill liner with its buff-coloured funnel and maybe a yellow-stacked Elder Dempster ship.

Author

IDOMENEUS
King George V Dock, 1972

Of course, the dock passed out of view before you were able to count the number of Alfred Holt Line ships, far less have time to identify the type or class. You could check up names later in the 'Herald' which published a daily list of arrivals and sailings, with a full list of ships berthed in the Clyde, on Mondays.

With the introduction of container services, however, the general cargo trade to King George V Dock began to decline and units of the vast Blue Funnel and Clan Line fleets were sold off. But although those two pruned their fleets radically there was still plenty to be seen in the dock in the early 1970's. With the closure of Queen's Dock and Prince's Dock the main centre for any general cargo on the Clyde was now based at 'KG Five'. As recently as 1973, on February 17th, you could have seen as many as eight ocean-going vessels berthed:–*Clan Menzies; City of London; Port St. Lawrence; Sea Explorer; Egori; Inventor; Raeburn; Dumbaia;* Clan and Blue Funnel though had lost the monopoly.

Author

KING GEORGE V DOCK, 1973

As the 1970's advanced, however, the dock became increasingly quiet and now lies almost deserted, the 1917 yards of quay empty. But it still provides the only general cargo berths on the Clyde and on a fairly recent occasion there were actually two large ships berthed there simultaneously. Both flew a foreign-flag which is not unusual in United Kingdom waters these days. One—the *Aristogenis*—was loading a general cargo for Venezuela, flew the Greek flag and was chartered through Hapag Lloyd and the Harrison Line. Astern was a large Kuwaiti but she owed her presence to a diversion from London caused by an industrial dispute. She was bound for the Persian Gulf and her cargo from Glasgow included valuable possessions of the Sultan of Oman.

Author

ARISTOGENIS & *IBN AL-BEITAR*
King George V Dock, 1983

Author

FLYING PHANTOM & *FLYING SCOUT*
Lying in an almost deserted King George V Dock, 1984

The only regular occupants of the dock now, might be a solitary tug tied up usually at the 'End Wall'; a Clyde Port Authority hopper or an East German trawler, transferring crews, berthed at the seaward end of the East Quay. According to the dock administrators it was very much a matter of 'Spot the Ship' in the mid-1980's and sadly, the last Clan liner to use the dock—*Clan Macgillivray*—wallowed down the Clyde, down to her marks, laden with machinery for Chittagong, in 1981...

London's Royal Victoria Dock was used in the Bank Holiday, August 1983, for power boat racing. Strathclyde Police practice their diving in King George V Dock, Glasgow.

Renfrew Ferry

The Renfrew Ferry is not strictly relevant to the theme of Glasgow Harbour, being outwith the boundary and neither connected with a quay nor dock. But it is fitting to conclude by recording the termination of this last, traditional trans-river service in June 1984.

**STRATHCLYDE REGIONAL COUNCIL
DEPARTMENT OF ROADS**

RENFREW FERRY

NOTICE is hereby given that following withdrawal of the Renfrew Ferry by the Clyde Port Authority on 31st May, 1984, Strathclyde Regional Council will introduce a PASSENGER ONLY FERRY on or about 1st July, 1984, operating continuously between 06 30 hrs and 09 30 hrs on seven days per week at the same location as the present ferry.

In the interval between closure of the present ferry and introduction of the new service a temporary replacement direct bus service will be operated between the Renfrew and Yoker ferry slips during the same hours as the new ferry service. This service will operate generally on a 30-minute frequency with 20-minute frequence at peak periods.

17th May, 1984.   M. S. McALONAN, Director.

The vehicular chain ferry had plied between Renfrew and Yoker since the late 19th century but its future had become somewhat insecure since the opening of the Clyde Tunnel. Operations are continued by a passenger launch.

Of course, most of the crossings have been uneventful and routine although there was a dramatic incident during World War II, involving the collision of two cargo ships in the immediate vicinity of the Ferry.

The Dutch vessel *Gaasterkerk* was proceeding down-river with tugs fore and aft. Ropner's *Clearpool* was inward-bound also in tow. As they approached Renfrew, the Ferry pulled away from Yoker slip—usually the Ferry waited until the River traffic passed before setting off.

Author

YOKER SWAN
Passenger-only replacement for Renfrew Ferry at Renfrew slip, 1984

Author

'RENFREW FERRY'—RENFREW
Laid-up Renfrew Harbour, 1984

Suddenly the *Gaasterkerk* sheered to port, possibly affected by a sudden current and her maierform bow struck the British ship, almost head-on and became firmly embedded in her hull. The *Gaasterkerk* immediately dropped an anchor which resulted in both chains[1] being completely dragged away from the Ferry. As the Ferry drifted up-river on the incoming tide, the crew attempted to arrest her progress by dropping anchor. Unfortunately as the anchors were rusty and seldom used, they refused to budge and remained firmly fixed to the Ferry's hull for some time. Meanwhile attention was being concentrated on the damaged vessels which were only separated after being burnt apart by oxy-acetylene torches.

At last the Ferry succeeded in anchoring herself in midstream but it was some two hours before a Clyde Navigation Trust craft arrived to take-off the passengers.

---

[1]   The chains of the Erskine Ferry were released at one end to allow the *Queen Elizabeth* to pass safely on 26th February, 1940

QUEEN'S DOCK, AS COMPLETED, 1880

J. F. Riddell (taken from *Clyde Navigation*)

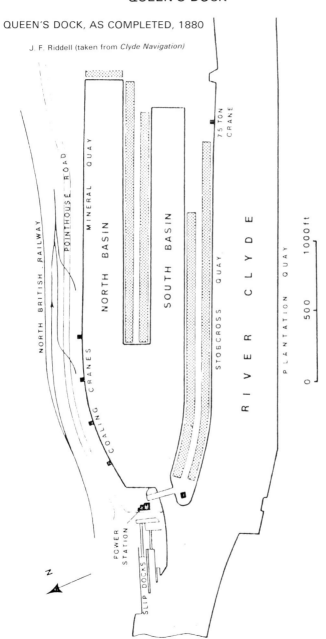

PRINCE'S DOCK, AS COMPLETED, 1897

J. F. Riddell (taken from *Clyde Navigation*)

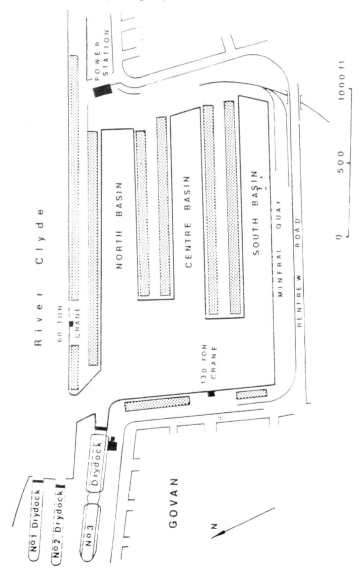

APPENDIX

Details of ships referred to in text and photographs

Name
Gross Tons/Year built

Owner — Disposal/Year

Administrator
8714/58

Harrison Line. *Oriental Sea*—78, Scrapped–79

Annan
955/07

Wm. Sloan & Co., Ltd. Scrapped—58

Aeneas
7641/47

Blue Funnel Line. Scrapped—72

*Alaunia**
7004/60

Cunard Steamship Co., Ltd. *Malancha*—69, *Huminastta*—70, *Yung Ming*—73, *Hong Qi No. 108*—75

*Albertwill**
13384/68

Triumph Shipping Corp.

Alsatia
7242/48

Cunard Steamship Co., Ltd. *Union Freedom*—63, Scrapped—77

American Importer
8228/45

United States Lines. *Interport*—71, Scrapped—72

Andria
7242/48

Cunard Steamship Co., Ltd. *Union Faith*—63, Wrecked, Total Loss—69

Antenor
7973/57

Blue Funnel Line. *Glenlochy*—70, *Dymas*—71, *Kaiyun*—73, Not registered 1985-86

*Anangel Might**
13889/78

Anangel Might Compania Naviera S.A.

*Antipolo I**
9004/69

Maritime Co. of the Philippines Inc. *Elke P*—85, *African Star*—85

*Arcadian**
3402/60

Ellerman Lines. *City of Famagusta*—74, *Batroun*—77

Ardchattan
284/07

J. & A. Gardner Ltd. Scrapped—54

*Aristogenis**
9989/80

Seafaith Bulk Carriers Corp.

*Artemis**
11982/77

Aramanios Corp.

Author
8715/58

Harrison Line. *Humber*—78, Scrapped—79

*Balmoral**
688/49

Waverley Excursions Ltd.

Barney Kirschbaum
7266/45

United States Government. Scrapped—72

113

Baron Inverclyde
5479/54

H. Hogarth & Sons Ltd. *John Maris*—63, *Saint John*—69, *Giannis*—70, Scrapped—72

Baskerville
5804/54

Runciman (London) Ltd. *Irolli*—67, *Glenealy*—70, Scrapped—74

*Baugnes**
13124/69

A/S Kristian Jebsens Rederi. *Westbon*—80

Baxtergate
6132/62

Turnbull Scott Shipping Co., Ltd. *Mediator*—71, *Mar Valiente*—72, Total Loss—81

Bhamo
5932/57

Henderson Line Ltd. *Bhamot*—79, Scrapped—79

*Blythswood**
786/63

Clyde Port Authority.

British Bombardier
32351/62

BP Tanker Co., Ltd. Scrapped—76

Brunes
10485/62

A/S Kristian Jebsens Rederi. *Marcus M.F.*—69, *Caribbean Dream*—81, *Sea Fury*—82, Scrapped—82

Caledonia
11255/48

Anchor Line Ltd. Scrapped—71

Caledonia
623/34

Caledonian Steam Packet Co., Ltd. *Old Caledonia*—71, Suffered extensive fire damage while floating restaurant & Scrapped—81

*Cape Franklin**
11815/59

Lyle Shipping Co., Ltd. *Vittorio Gardella*—75

Cape Howe
19032/62

Lyle Shipping Co., Ltd. *Al Tawwab*—78, Scrapped—84

Captain Cook (ex Letitia)
13475/25

New Zealand Government. Scrapped—60

Cavtat
2092/68

Atlantiska Plovidba. Wrecked & Total Loss—74

Celtic Star
5575/18

Blue Star Line Ltd. Torpedoed & Sunk 29/3/43

*Cerium**
532/43

Imperial Chemical Industries Ltd. *G.R. Velie*—67, *G.B. Church*—76

*Chieftain**
223/30

Steel & Bennie Ltd. *St. Eval*—68

Cilicia
11157/37

Anchor Line Ltd. *Jan Backx*—66, Scrapped—80

Circassia
11170/37

Anchor Line Ltd. Scrapped—66

City of Coventry
7568/49

Ellerman Lines. *Ingrid*—67, *Annie*—69, Scrapped—70

City of London
8434/47

Ellerman Lines. *Sanda N*—66, Scrapped—68

*City of London**
9793/70

Ellerman Lines. *Sea Lord*—82

City of Ottawa
7622/50

Ellerman Lines. *City of Leeds*—71, *Gulf Venture*—75, Scrapped—77

City of Oxford
7593/48

Ellerman Lines. *Union Arabia*—75, Scrapped—78

City of Philadelphia 7591/49	Ellerman Lines. *Kapto Spyro*—67, *Spyro*—70, Scrapped—71
City of Swansea 9959/46	Ellerman Lines. *Benkitlan*—68, Scrapped—72
Clan Colquoun 7914/18	Clan Line Steamers Ltd. *Ionnis Livanos*—47, *Jenny*—48, *Iman Bondjol*—52, *D J Atineera*—53, Scrapped—56
Clan Forbes 7568/38	Clan Line Steamers Ltd. Scrapped—59
Clan Grant 9322/62	Clan Line Steamers Ltd. *Enriquetta*—80, Scrapped—84
Clan Macgillivray 8811/62	Clan Line Steamers Ltd. *Clan Macboyd*—81, Scrapped—84
*Clan Menzies** 7553/58	Clan Line Steamers Ltd. *Trinity Splendour*—79, *Xing Kong*—80
Clan Shaw 8101/50	Clan Line Steamers Ltd. *Steenbock*—60, *South African Seafarer*—66, Wrecked, Total Loss—66
Claymore 776/1881	David MacBrayne Ltd. Scrapped—31
*Colina** 1776/60	Donaldson Line Ltd. *Andrew B Crosbie*—67, *Aktian*—76
Contest 213/33	William Watkins Ltd. Scrapped—72
Corinaldo 3392/49	Donaldson Line Ltd. *Ningpo*—67, *Kinaros*—67, Scrapped—80
Corinthian 3198/38	Ellerman Lines. Scrapped—63
Corinthic 15682/47	Shaw Savill Line. Scrapped—69
Crane 800/37	General Steam Navigation Co., Ltd. *Nissos Sifnos*—64, *Toula*—69, *Al Madani*—75, Wrecked, Total Loss—80
Cumberland 11281/48	Federal Steam Navigation Co., Ltd. Scrapped—76
*Cypress** 12035/58	Wilson Shipping Corp. Ltd. *Union*—68, *Freja*—69, *Scotiacliffe Hall*—72, *Scotiacliffe*—75, *Navifor Norse*—76
*Dalmarnock** 2266/70	Strathclyde Regional Council.
Doric 10674/49	Shaw Savill Line. Scrapped—69
Doulos (ex *Franca C*)* 6806/14	Doulos Ltd.
Dumbaia 6564/60	Elder Dempster Lines Ltd. Scrapped—84
Earl of Skye 37985/65	Earlot Ltd. Scrapped—84

Egori 8586/57	Elder Dempster Lines Ltd. *Azza*—78, Scrapped—79
Elysia 6499/65	Anchor Line. *Armanistan*—69, *Strathavoch*—75, *Sharp Island*—78, Scrapped—83
Empire Puma 7777/20	British Ministry of Shipping (Lyle Shipping-Managers) *Inchwells*—47, *Point Clear*—51, *Giacomo Paggio*—52, *Enrichetto*—54, *Silvana*—58, Scrapped—59
Eurofreighter* 30909/71	Seatrain Lines Inc. *Seapac Valley Forge*—81, *Oriental Knight*—81
Fair Head 1573/57	Head Line. *Maldive Sea*—75, Scrapped—83
Ferncourt 9918/38	Fearnley & Eger. *Amilcar*—54, *Daisy*—57, Scrapped—64
Flying Dipper* 274/58	Clyde Shipping Co., Ltd. *Pamela Joy*—77
Flying Fulmar* 298/74	Clyde Shipping Co., Ltd.
Flying Merlin 261/51	Clyde Shipping Co., Ltd. *Possente*—67, Scrapped—78
Flying Phantom* 347/81	Clyde Shipping Co., Ltd.
Flying Scout* 290/70	Clyde Shipping Co., Ltd.
Forager 244/44	Steel & Bennie Ltd. *Mastino*—63, Scrapped—84
Frisian Express* 475/57	Vroon's Handel & Scheepv. Orderneering N.V.
Gaasterkerk 8373/22	United Netherlands Navigation Co. Torpedoed & Sunk 1942
Glasgow (HMS)*† 3500/79	Royal Navy.
Glen Shiel 195/59	Hay Hamilton Ltd. Sank & Total Loss—73
Grand Encounter* 16380/72	Blackwall Shipping Corp. *Laurentian Forest*—85
Gundula 1039/54	Gloria Reederi Grapel & Co., *Karim*—65, Sank & Total Loss—72
Haparangi 11281/47	New Zealand Shipping Co., Ltd. Scrapped—73
Hasselo 8490/39	Ragnar Kallstrom. *Hassel*—67, Scrapped—67
Hazelmoor 5572/54	Walter Runciman & Co., Ltd. *Freddie*—78, Scrapped—78
Hebrides 585/98	David MacBrayne Ltd. Scrapped—55
Hereford Express 497/50	Rederij M.S. "Margot". Wrecked & Total Loss—70
Hertford 11276/48	Federal Steam Navigation Co., Ltd. *Thia Despina*—75, *Georghios Frangakis*—78, Scrapped, after lay-up since 78,—84

Hinakura 11272/49	New Zealand Shipping Co., Ltd. Scrapped—74
Hopper No. 26 941/54	Clyde Port Authority. Scrapped—84
Hopper No. 27* 981/62	Clyde Port Authority.
Hororata 12090/42	New Zealand Shipping Co., Ltd. *Nor*—67, Scrapped—67
Hurunui 11276/48	New Zealand Shipping Co., Ltd. Scrapped—73
Ibn Al Beitar* 15446/77	United Arab Shipping Co.
Idomeneus 7413/49	Blue Funnel Line. *Gulf Voyager*—76, Scrapped—78
Inventor 9171/64	Harrison Line. *Penta World*—81, Scrapped—85
Irish Coast* 3824/52	Coast Lines Ltd. *Orpheus*—68, *Semi Ramis II*—69, *Achilleus*—69, *Apollon 11*—69, *Regency*—81
Irish Spruce* 39773/83	Irish Shipping Ltd.
Itapui* 10846/71	Cia. De Nav. Lloyd Brasileiro.
Jalaveera 5074/58	Scindia S.N. Co., Ltd. *Al Salma*—78, Scrapped—84
Jason 10160/50	Blue Funnel Line. Scrapped—72
Jevington Court 6248/56	Court Line Ltd. *Krishna Jayanti*—63, *Shankara*—74, Scrapped—75
Johanna Buitelaar 496/52	Rederij Buitelaar N.V. *Lincoln Express*—76, Scrapped—82
Kantara 3213/47	Moss Hutchison Line. *Constantos II*—72, Scrapped—80
King Edward 502/01	Caledonian Steam Packet Co., Ltd. Scrapped—52
Kong Haakon VII 7068/42	Royal Norwegian Government. *Cavofrigelo*—51, *Emporios*—53, *Aguinaldo*—67, *Liberty Three*—69, Scrapped—72
King Charles 5993/57	King Line Ltd. *Aegis Might*—73, Scrapped—79
Kirriemoor 22198/65	Walter Runciman & Co., Ltd. *Al Tahir*—78, Scrapped—84
Lairds Ben 995/49	Burns & Laird Lines Ltd. *Brookmount*—59, *Ikaria*—70, *Pierre Rodolphe*—71, *Ziad*—73, *Sweet Waves*—79, Shelled, Sunk, Lebanon, Total Loss—83
Lairdsburn 1870/23	Burns & Laird Lines. Scrapped—54
Lairdscrest 789/36	Burns & Laird Lines. *San Marco*—69, *Kronos*—75, Not registered 1981-82
Lairdsfox* 562/52	Burns & Laird Lines. *Lilaida*—77

Lairdsglen 1544/54	Burns & Laird Lines. *Devon Express*—74, Scrapped—83
Lairdshill 1679/21	Burns & Laird Lines. Scrapped—57
Lairds Loch 1736/44	Burns & Laird Lines. *Hey Daroma*—69, Total Loss—70
Lairdsrose 1151/02	Burns Laird Lines. Scrapped—49
Lancaster 4949/58	Lancaster Shipping Co., S.A. Scrapped—81
Laurentia 8249/45	Donaldson Line Ltd. Scrapped—67
Leandros 10183/63	Astromerito Compania Naviera S.A. *Filadelfos*—74, *Fourkero II*—81, Wrecked & Total Loss—81
Lennox II 795/54	Clyde Port Authority. Scrapped—83
Letitia 4667/61	Donaldson Line. *Bibi*—67, *Tepic*—77, *Tepora*—84, Total Loss—84
*Lion** 3333/67	Burns & Laird Lines. *Baroness M*—85
Lismoria 8323/45	Donaldson Line. *Neon*—67, Scrapped—67
Livanita 18736/62	A/S Uglands Rederi. *Vida*—78, *Hoppet*—84, Scrapped—84
Loch Ard 611/55	David MacBrayne Ltd. *Holborn*—71, *Candiera*—76, Sank & Total Loss—84
Lochbroom 1086/1871	David MacBrayne Ltd. Acquired by MacBrayne 1931 Scrapped—37
Lochbroom 325/46	David MacBrayne Ltd. *Focomar*—72, Sank & Total Loss—74
Loch Carron 683/51	David MacBrayne Ltd. *Georgis K*—77, Not Registered 1984-85
*Lochdunvegan** 528/46	David MacBrayne Ltd. *Fanis*—73, *Vassilis*—76
Lochgarry 1670/98	David MacBrayne Ltd. Total Loss—42
Lochgorm 635/96	David MacBrayne Ltd. Scrapped—51
Lycaon 7859/54	Blue Funnel Line. *Glaucus*—76, *United Vanguard*—77, Wrecked & Total Loss—79
Malancha 8195/37	Brocklebank Line. *Malan*—62, Scrapped—62
Manchester Trader 7363/41	Manchester Liners Ltd. Scrapped—63
Maskeliya 7350/54	Brocklebank Line. *Ocean Joy*—69, Scrapped—72
Maturata 7365/55	Brocklebank Line. *Maldive Explorer*—69, *Lanka Sinna*—70, *Ocean Fruit*—70, *Apai Samut*—72, Scrapped—72

*Melbrook** 11075/64	Hall Bros. S.S. Co., Ltd. *Exmoor*—72, *Annita*—78, *Anthi Marina*—85
*Melete** 35489/75	Neptune Maritime Co.
Memphis 3575/47	Moss Hutchison Line Ltd. *Elias*—72, Scrapped—81
*Mona's Isle** 4657/66	Isle of Man Steam Packet Co. Ltd. *Al Fahad*—86
Nea Hellas 16991/22	Greek Line. *New York*—54, Scrapped—61
Neddy (ex T.E. Tanker). 14304/43-62	Lavta Corp. *Omnium Mariner*—73, Scrapped—78
Nestor 7802/52	Blue Funnel Line. *Glenaffric*—69, *Orestes*—70, *Aegis Dignity*—71, Scrapped—73
*Newshot** 799/43	Clyde Navigation Trust. *Iona-B*—74
Niceto de Larrinaga 10520/59	Larrinaga S.S. Co., Ltd. *Aegis Bounty*—72, *Char Chun*—78, *Char Cheng*—81, Not registered 1984-85
Niger Palm 5202/48	Palm Line Ltd. *Triaina*—66, Scrapped—68
Ocean Cock 182/32	William Watkins Ltd. Scrapped—69
*Orfeo** 12994/64	Soc. Ligure Di Armamento. *Saudi Spirit*—84, *Hector*—84, *Tanna*—84, *Akbar*—84
Pacific Unity 9511/48	Furness Withy & Co., Ltd. *Lavrentios*—64, Scrapped—70
*Paula de Aspe** 689/56	Benjamin Suarez Garcia. *Magali*—65
*Pibroch** 157/57	Glenlight Shipping Ltd.
*Pioneer** 1071/74	Caledonian MacBrayne Ltd.
Polyphemus 7414/48	Blue Funnel Line. *Asphalion*—72, *Gulf Anchor*—75, Scrapped—79
Port Brisbane 12684/49	Port Line Ltd. Scrapped—75
Port Launceston 8957/57	Port Line Ltd. *United Vantage*—77, Scrapped—80
Port St. Lawrence 9040/61	Port Line Ltd. *Matangi*—75, *Nordave*—82, Scrapped—83
*Prometheus** 12094/67	Blue Funnel Line. *Oriental Merchant*—79
Queen Elizabeth 83673/40	Cunard Steamship Co., Ltd. *The Elizabeth*—69, *Seawise University*—70, Fire & Total Loss—72
Queen Mary 81237/36	Cunard Steamship Co., Ltd. Sold to city of Long Beach, Calif.—67
*Queen Mary II** 881/33	Caledonian Steam Packet Co., Ltd. *Queen Mary*—76, Sold—83 and to be floating restaurant on the Thames

Racia 163/30	William Watkins Ltd. Scrapped—69
Raeburn 6274/57	Lamport & Holt Line Ltd. *Braeburn*—79, Scrapped—79
Renfrew /35	Glasgow Corporation. *Erskine*—62, Withdrawn from service—71
Renfrew* 170/52	Strathclyde Regional Council. Withdrawn from service—84
Robert M* 1593/70	Coe Metcalf Shipping Ltd.
Rounton Grange* 40753/72	Furness Withy & Co., Ltd. *China Marquis*—84
Royal Scotsman 3288/36	Burns & Laird Lines Ltd. *Apollo*—67, Scrapped—84
Royal Ulsterman 3290/36	Burns & Laird Lines Ltd. *Cammel Laird*—68, *Sounion*—70, Shelled, Sunk, Lebanon, Total Loss—73
Saint Fergus 346/64	J. & A. Gardner Ltd. *Cape Elizabeth*—81, Scrapped—83
Saint Kentigern 249/38	J. & A. Gardner Ltd. Scrapped—63
Saint Modan* 488/60	J. & A. Gardner Ltd. *Modan*—79, *Nialed*—81, *Monique*—82, *Nadir*—84
Saint Oran 249/23	J. & A. Gardner Ltd. Scrapped—54
Santona 3218/59	Donaldson Line Ltd. *Maldive Trader*—74, Scrapped—83
Scan Trader* 2539/60	Circle Shipping Ltd.
Scottish Coast* 3817/57	Burns & Laird Lines Ltd. *Galaxias*—69
Sea Explorer 9164/59	Mariana Navigation S.A. *New Sea Explorer*—82, Scrapped—83
Sidonia 5744/61	Anchor Line Ltd. *Hupeh*—67, *Sun Opal*—82, Scrapped—85
Sir Galahad (Logistic Landing Ship) 4473/66	Ministry of Defence. Falklands, Total loss—82
Sound of Sanda* 275/38	Western Ferries Ltd.
Specialist 7263/43	Harrison Line. *Mitera*—64, Scrapped—68
Succour (Coastal Salvage Vessel) 775/43	Royal Fleet Auxiliary. Scrapped—73
Suevic 13587/50	Shaw Savill Line. Scrapped—74
Sun XI* 183/25	W. H. J. Alexander Ltd. *Schelde*—64, *Andrea*—65
Sun XV 183/25	W. H. J. Alexander Ltd. Scrapped—69

Sunima*
3825/58
Karl J B Staubo. *Mulde*—64, *Cefallonian Grace*—79, *Ionian Grace*—82

Sussex (HMS)†
9830/29
Royal Navy. Scrapped—50

Tarry
1876/58
Compania Maritime Laguna. Scrapped—84

Theseus
7561/55
Blue Funnel Line. *Aegis Myth*—71, *Aegis Care*—72, Scrapped—73

Thetis*
35513/74
Neptune Maritime Co.

Thunderer*
208/58
Steel & Bennie Ltd. *Plymgarth*—73, *Ierex*—81

Trojan
90/05
J. & J. Hay. Scrapped—53

Trojan Star
9257/16
Blue Star Line Ltd. Scrapped—59

Varna
1514/21
Glen & Co., Ltd. Bombed & finally sank—41

Vehicular Ferryboat No. 4
275/38
Clyde Navigation Trust. Scrapped—77

Vishva Bandhan*
9983/74
Shipping Corporation of India.

Warrior
259/35
Steel & Bennie Ltd. *St. Agnes*—69, Withdrawn from service—84, Scrapped—85

Wasp (USS)†
14700/40
United States Navy. Torpedoed & Sunk—42

Waverley*
693/47
Caledonian Steam Packet Co., Ltd. Owners— Waverley Steam Navigation Co., Ltd.—75

Wellington Star
11994/52
Blue Star Line Ltd. *Hawkes Bay*—75, Scrapped—79

Winga
2234/57
Glen & Co., Ltd. *Radiant*—66, Sank & Total Loss—78

Yewhill*
1089/57
John Stewart & Co., Ltd. *Silverthorn*—74, *Minas-Cue*—78

Yewmount*
1031/55
John Stewart & Co., Ltd. *Elias G*—74, *Atlantis I*—81

Yoma
8137/58
Henderson Line Ltd. *Daru*—67, *Anjo One*—80, *Lone Eagle*—79, Scrapped—82

* Registered with Lloyd's 1985-86/under new ownership and registered with Lloyd's 1985-86
† Standard tons displacement

Index